Contents

To my wife, Pamela, our children, Daniel and Emma, and grandson, who is the solution to one of the clues

THE TIMES

HOW TO MASTER THE TIMES CROSSWORD

The Times
Cryptic Crossword
Demystified

TIM MOOREY

TIMES
BOOKS

HarperCollinsPublishers
77-85 Fulham Palace Road
Hammersmith, London
W6 8JB

www.collins.co.uk

Collins is a registered trademark of HarperCollinsPublishers Ltd

First published in 2008

Copyright © Tim Moorey 2008

14 13 12 11 10 09 08

7 6 5 4 3 2 1

A catalogue record for this book is available from the British Library

ISBN 978-0-00-727784-1

Printed and bound in Great Britain by Clays Ltd, St Ives plc.

Layout by Susie Bell.

Mixed Sources

Product group from well-managed
forests and other controlled sources
www.fsc.org Cert no. SW-COC-1806
© 1996 Forest Stewardship Council

FSC is a non-profit international organisation established to promote the
responsible management of the world's forests. Products carrying the FSC
label are independently certified to assure consumers that they come
from forests that are managed to meet the social, economic and
ecological needs of present and future generations.

Find out more about HarperCollins and the environment at
www.harpercollins.co.uk/green

Foreword

In a recent nationwide poll to select icons of Britain, *The Times* Crossword was nominated, alongside such other well-loved features of our national life as Rolls Royce, the Routemaster bus, Test Match Special, and (perhaps appropriately) Sherlock Holmes and the *Oxford English Dictionary*. I suspect many people who never attempt to solve them still identify crosswords as a peculiarly British form of intelligent recreation, the modern incarnation as it were of the riddling word games enjoyed by our forebears, and of the puns and jokes to which our language is so well suited, with its many synonyms and its short words that make such simple and versatile playthings.

Although the crossword itself is an American invention, it took its particular cryptic form over here, and *The Times* Crossword (tackled then as now by 'Top People', as the advertising campaign used to put it) quickly established its reputation as the leader in its field, the more baffling of the day's clues regularly the subject of anxious committee work in the corridors of Whitehall, and the completed grid (were one to be achieved) a trophy to be displayed casually on one's desk.

In those days, our crossword was truly hard, as can be seen if one attempts one from the Times Online archive. Many clues then were vague references rather than today's precision tools, sometimes even without definitions of the answer; anagrams and other tricks were often not indicated; and a fearsome knowledge of the byways of English literature was necessary to complete each day's puzzle.

But things have long moved on from those elitist days. Edmund Akenhead, as editor in the 1970s, established our modern principle of fairness: that every clue should lead unambiguously to its answer, that it should contain a proper definition, and that the word-play should be grammatically accurate. He also introduced a well-designed set of grids with all the answers having half of their letters cross-checking with others, so that solvers could get reasonable help towards a recalcitrant clue.

We have retained and built on these principles since then, as our aim, contrary to what some may think, is not to baffle and annoy solvers, but to give them an interesting, varied, and worthwhile daily challenge which we hope many will rise successfully to. The old-style Eng-Lit obstacle course has passed away, and we aim to provide a puzzle which reasonably intelligent and educated solvers (typical *Times* readers, in fact) can hope to complete in a half-hour-or-so train journey without needing to annoy their fellow-travellers in the quiet carriage by beeping into the electronic aids on their mobiles. Indeed, one of my principles as editor is always to strike out any clue, however brilliant its idea, that can only be expressed in a lengthy and awkward way, and to replace it with something simple and elegant, even if it is much easier. As one of my predecessors, John Grant, used to say, ideally every clue should be a sentence that could plausibly be uttered in real life; if it 'could only be a crossword clue', out it goes.

So *The Times* Crossword (and its Saturday jumbo offspring) is certainly not the hardest puzzle around; much harder ones appear in the weekend papers and magazines, which use unfamiliar vocabulary and which may require the solver to identify a theme, to decode clues before starting to solve them, or to manipulate answers before writing them in. Our puzzle, on the other hand, has no themes or extra complications; one of its delights lies in the way that the clues read like normal sentences, but turn out on examination actually to lead to something totally different. (Indeed, I have continually to remind the subeditors at *The Times*, who want to apply their style guide to our formulations, that our clues are not real sentences but code, and may be ruined by the alteration of even a single letter.) I think of our setters as conjurors, who hide things in broad daylight and distract you from seeing them by cleverly diverting your attention. But the answers should not be obscure, and one of the satisfactions of solving is the feeling that one has been quite legitimately deceived, and should have realised what was going on much sooner.

So I welcome this opportunity to encourage all who want to improve their solving ability, or to enjoy our puzzles for the first time, and I warmly commend Tim's practical and comprehensive guide, which will give you all you need to join our large company of devotees.

Richard Browne
Crossword Editor of *The Times*

Introduction

Do you need this book? Anyone who has been solving *The Times* Crossword successfully for a long time has picked up all the necessary knowledge, maybe after years of trial and error, and reached a stage where no thinking, solving methods, clue types and so on are needed. This person simply completes the puzzle each day.

If you are reading this book, it is likely that you are not yet at this advanced level. However, it is possible to improve your solving skills with suitable instruction, as I know from running crossword workshops in various parts of the UK.

Is this book only for beginners?

Not at all, it is also for anyone wanting to master crossword puzzles so he or she isn't regularly left with unfinished clues before the next day's newspaper arrives. This book should also appeal to another group: those who nearly always manage to complete the puzzle but wish to do so in less time.

Why have I written this book?

I'd like to offer three qualifications:

1. A (not very fast) *Times* solver, on and off for over 50 years.
2. A crossword setter for the *Sunday Times*, *The Week* magazine and other national media for nearly 20 years.
3. A tutor of crossword workshops for the past 10 years.

It is thanks to this teaching experience that I am able to write about cryptic crosswords and how to solve them. Having seen many solvers grapple with puzzles on my workshops, I'm well aware of the many points that can trip up beginners as well as more experienced solvers.

The book's focus

The focus of this book is firmly on the solver. I have consulted a fair number of solver friends, former colleagues and acquaintances, all of whose experience and techniques are incorporated throughout the book. Although my emphasis is also on practicality, I would not wish to be seen as laying down rules on solving; there are really no such things. Ultimately, everyone finds their own way of doing crosswords and my hope is that I help you to find yours, and that you will adopt and reject the tips according to whether they suit you.

XIMENES AND AZED

Having taken his name from a Grand Inquisitor in the Spanish Inquisition, Ximenes (Derrick Macnutt) was long-term setter of a crossword puzzle in the Observer. He is remembered today, not just for his puzzles, but also because he set out fair and consistent principles for cryptic crosswords and especially clues, in a ground-breaking 1966 book *Ximenes on the Art of the Crossword*. His successor Azed (Jonathan Crowther whose pseudonym originates from another Grand Inquisitor, Archbishop of Seville and patron of Christopher Columbus) and the majority of setters today in national media, including the Times, follow virtually all 'Ximenean' principles.

Puzzles for practice

I follow the well-established teaching principle that adults learn best by doing rather than reading or being lectured to. So I have included lots of practice clues and puzzles, with detailed notes explaining the solutions to each clue and puzzle. These should leave you in no doubt about why the solutions are what they are. Finally, the full index is designed to encourage the book's continual use as a manual, rather than a book that you read once and then donate to Oxfam.

Misapprehensions and what is required

There are many misapprehensions about *The Times* Crossword, such as that you require a good knowledge of rare words, literature and the classics. Many tell me that the puzzle would be better without quotations when, in fact, they have not featured for many years!

What sort of knowledge is needed?

The stated intention is that *The Times* Crossword can be done by any moderately well-educated person with a love of language and problem-solving, without recourse to reference books. However, this was not always the case, as Richard Browne, the current *Times* crossword editor, explained in *The Times* on the puzzle's 75th anniversary:

'Everything evolves,' he wrote. 'Twenty years ago setters could confidently expect that most solvers would have a reasonable acquaintance with the principal plays of Shakespeare, the main characters and events in the Bible, probably a bit of Milton, a few lyric verses, Dickens perhaps, certainly Sherlock Holmes and some staples of the Victorian nursery such as Lear and Lewis Carroll, and you could confidently clue a word just with a reference. That doesn't work any more, partly because the world has widened up so much.

'We have lots of people in this country now from different backgrounds – India, Africa, America, whatever – who have a different system of education, and of course we have people logging on worldwide to *Times Online*, doing the crossword. So it's a larger and more varied audience – you're no longer talking exclusively to the public-school, Oxbridge types who were the core of your readership 50 or 60 years ago.'

Why do *The Times* Cryptic?

> *'I always do the crossword first thing in the morning, to see if I've enough marbles left to make it worth my while getting up.'*
> Letter to *The Times* from an elderly reader

There is indeed scientific evidence that tackling any crossword can be good for you. Medical research continues to support the notion that mental exercise from activities such as crosswords is beneficial, especially in later life, and stimulates the brain. A New York neurologist, Doctor Joe Verghese, conducted research in this area for over 21 years and found that those who kept their minds nimble were 75 per cent less likely to develop dementia or Alzheimer's disease.

'Do something that is mentally challenging to you,' he has said. 'It seems that remaining mentally agile makes the brain more healthy and more likely to resist illness, just as physical exercise can protect the body from disease.'

Are crosswords educational? Yes, in the sense that they can do wonders for your vocabulary and general knowledge, particularly when you are introduced to a new reference or subject.

Is this book relevant to other crosswords?

It is specific to *The Times* with many references to its style and with 'Tips for *The Times*' throughout. Nonetheless, many of the techniques recommended do apply to a greater or lesser extent to other daily and weekend cryptics such as those in the *Independent*, *Daily Telegraph*, the *Financial Times*, the *Daily Express* and perhaps less so, the *Guardian*.

Clues and puzzles in this book

Examples of clues are virtually all from *The Times* and have been chosen not only to illuminate explanations but also to demonstrate the best in clueing standards for which *The Times* is noted. Indeed many have appeared as the 'Clue of The Week', a feature of *The Week* magazine for the past ten years.

The practice puzzles are all from *The Times*, mostly of recent vintage. I have tried to select ones with varying levels of difficulty and many clues to savour.

PART 1

CROSSWORD BASICS

1: Terminology

'She had another look at The Times *Crossword. The clues might as well have been written in a foreign language.'* Simon Brett, *The Stabbing in the Stables*

This first chapter establishes the terms used throughout. It is essential reading for beginners, and those solvers who already attempt the crossword should find it useful to have the different clue types explained.

What is a cryptic clue?

This may seem an unnecessary question but I know from the crossword workshops that not everyone has a clear understanding of this.

> A cryptic clue is a sentence or phrase, involving a degree of deception, making sense and frequently conjuring an image, or triggering thoughts, in its surface reading, but when read in another way can be decoded using a limited number of well-established techniques to give a solution. Thus 'cryptic' is used in its meaning of hidden or misleading.

These are the other terms we shall use:

- Answers to **clues**, running across and down are entered into a **grid**, popularly a diagram, which has **across** and **down** slots.
- The **grid** in the case of *The Times* Crossword contains black square **blocks**, hence it's a **blocked** puzzle.
- One crossword in *The Times* on Saturdays almost always has a grid with **bars** rather than blocks. This is the *Times/Listener*, which is an example of a **barred** puzzle.
- Clue answers are variously called **solutions**, **entries** and indeed **answers**.
- Where a solution letter, or letters, is able to be confirmed by intersecting entries, they are **checked** letters. **Unchecked** letters (**unches** in the trade) are therefore the opposite: the solver has no second way of confirming them.

- The person responsible for the crossword is a **setter**; more commonly, but in a term less attractive to most crossword professionals, a **compiler**.
- The North American term **constructor**, which suits puzzles with difficult-to-build grids and a mere semblance of crypticity, is not used much elsewhere.
- Other terms associated with clues such as **wordplay**, **anagram** and **anagram fodder** are explained as we meet them.

For completeness, there is another rarely used crossword term – **light** – whose meaning has fluctuated somewhat from the early days of crosswords but is defined by the *Collins English Dictionary* today as the solution to a clue.

2: Overview of Clues and Indicators

'The question is,' said Alice, 'whether you can make words mean so many different things.' Lewis Carroll, *Through the Looking Glass*

In this chapter I provide a short overview of the basics of clues and how to recognize them. Detailed points on each clue type are the subject of Chapter 3.

Characteristics of a cryptic clue

We will consider twelve types of cryptic clue, of which the majority conform to the principles contained in this image:

CRYPTIC CLUES (MOSTLY) HAVE TWO PARTS

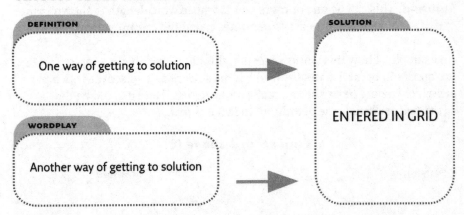

Either the definition or the wordplay can come first in the clue sentence; and either could be exploited first to obtain the solution. Whichever does come second in your solving order acts as confirmation that you have the correct solution.

Taking each element in turn:

Definition: The definition can
  • take the form of a word, or words in a phrase

- be an example of the solution (e.g. *fruit* can be defined as *apple, perhaps*)
- be a (misleadingly expressed) synonym of the solution. To this end, definitions are often words that have more than one meaning

TIP FOR THE TIMES
In my experience, beginners find it much easier to decode a cryptic clue when they are told that the **definition** is almost always either at the beginning or end of the clue sentence or phrase.

Wordplay: This is the way to elicit the solution if the definition does not do so. It can be seen as either:
- the letters of the solution needing manipulation in one of several ways to provide another indication of the definition, *or*
- individual word or words in the clue having to be interpreted in a different way from the surface meaning

Perhaps strictly accurately the terms should be **word** and **letterplay**.

Solution: This can be one or more words whose word-length is shown at the end of the clue in parentheses (sometimes called the **enumeration**).

An example of how this works is seen in this clue which has a simple juxtaposition of three parts from which the solver has to discover which parts are which, before he or she can make any progress. Here it could be that either *find* or *above* is the definition. In fact it is *find*.

Find record above (8)

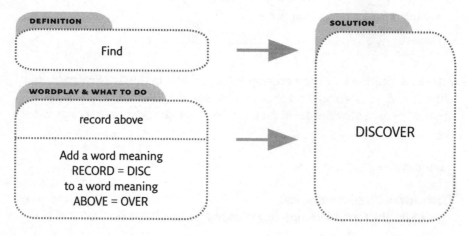

DEFINITION

Find

WORDPLAY & WHAT TO DO

record above

Add a word meaning
RECORD = DISC
to a word meaning
ABOVE = OVER

SOLUTION

DISCOVER

Linkwords: Few clues are as straightforward in construction as the previous example and the first mild challenge is that there is often a linkword between the two parts to give the solution. The chart then is:

CRYPTIC CLUES WITH LINKING WORDS

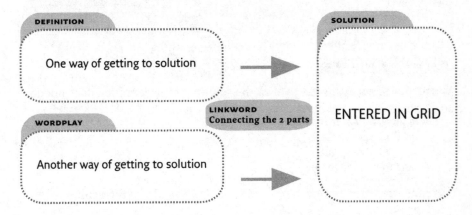

Below is a clue which also starts with the definition but, in addition, has a linkword, one that is commonly used: *in*. The sense conveyed by *in* is that a synonym for church house can be formed from the two parts *earlier* and *years* (if the latter is taken as an abbreviation).

Church house in earlier years (6)

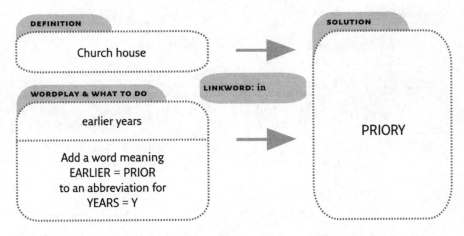

Next is an example in which the definition is the final word in the clue and in which the linkword is also *in*, the sense being that the wordplay is *seen in* the solution. This is a trickier clue than we have seen so far, as the solution *tea service* is split into two parts, *teaser* and *vice*, to form the wordplay.

Puzzle failing in China (3, 7)

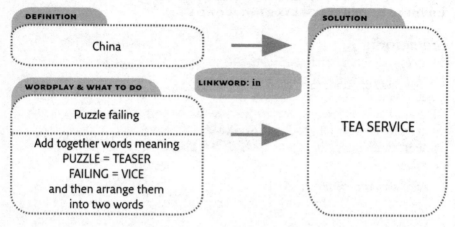

As well as linkwords between definition and wordplay, there can also be similar linkage within the wordplay to connect its different parts. Here it is *and*, a simple additive indication. The other linkword *is* indicates that the definition can be formed from the wordplay.

ADDITIVE CLUE: What babies need is sleep and food (7)

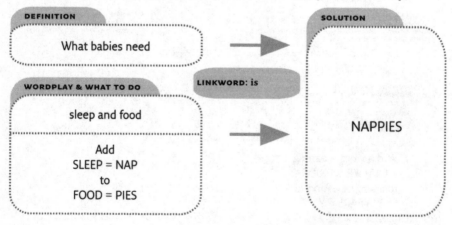

You will notice that the last of the example clues is labelled *additive*. In fact all so far have been of this type, a relatively plain construction of A + B = C which we shall consider later in more detail as one of the twelve clue types, dividing these into one group of eight and one group of four. Why split clues into two groups? Because some always contain the means of identifying their type (the first eight) and others virtually always do not (the remaining four). This distinction is amplified in the section which follows.

Indicators

Complete beginners on my workshops often say something like this:

'Yes, I know that there are different types of clue but how on earth do I know which is which?'

The answer is as follows. For the **first group of eight** there is always a signpost to the solution, called the indicator, within the clue sentence. Remember, an indicator is the means of identifying clue types. In Chapter 3 we will consider the specific indicators for the first group of eight clue types. The example clue below shows how indicators work. The indicator here is *wrong*, showing that this is an **anagram** clue. The concept behind this indicator is that the letters to be mixed are incorrect and must be changed to form the solution. There are many ways of giving the same anagram instruction to solvers, as you will see in Chapter 3.

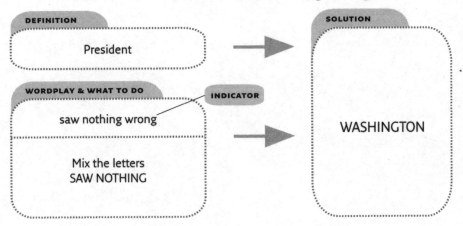

ANAGRAM CLUE: President saw nothing wrong (10)

DEFINITION
President

SOLUTION

WORDPLAY & WHAT TO DO
saw nothing wrong

INDICATOR

Mix the letters
SAW NOTHING

WASHINGTON

For the **remaining group of four**, it's usually a case of informed guesswork rather than indicators. This may seem unreasonable and impossible for the novice solver but I aim to prove that this is not really the case.

In the meantime, this may be a good time to point out that trial and error and/or inspired guesswork are part and parcel of good solving. This is reinforced by the clueing practice of all *Times* setters whereby the clue type will nearly always become clear on working backwards from the solutions. Indeed, when a solver sees the solution the following day, he or she should only rarely be left thinking (as Ximenes put it):

'I thought of that but I couldn't see how it could be right.'

We will now proceed to examine in detail all clue types and their indicators, with one and sometimes two examples of each type.

3: Clue Types and Indicators in Detail

'Give us a kind of clue.' W.S. Gilbert, *Utopia Limited*

Until Chapter 8, we'll keep it simple with regard to clue types. In later chapters we will see that the clue types can and often do overlap, involving more than one sort of manipulation of letters or words within any one clue.

The first eight clue types

We will now examine each of the eight clue types in detail, together with their indicators, and offer some example clues. To give yourself solving practice, you may wish from now on to cover up the bottom half of the diagram that contains the solution and wordplay.

The first eight types are shown in the circular chart below, and we shall take each in turn, working clockwise from the top.

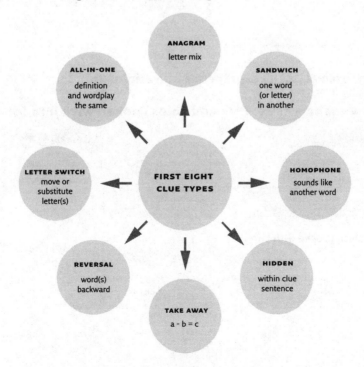

1. The anagram clue

An **anagram**, sometimes termed a **letter mix**, is a rearrangement of letters or words within the clue sentence to form the solution word or words. The letters to be mixed (the **anagram fodder**) may or may not include an abbreviation, a routine trick for old hands but, as I have observed, a cause of some discomfort for first-timers. Later, we shall see examples of abbreviations within clues but for the time being the examples do not have abbreviations:

ANAGRAM CLUE: Mum, listen for a change (6)

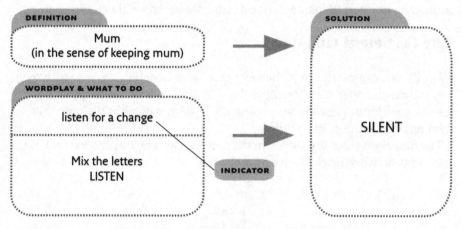

This next example is an **anagram** clue with a **linkword**:

ANAGRAM CLUE: Fish and chips cooked with lard (9)

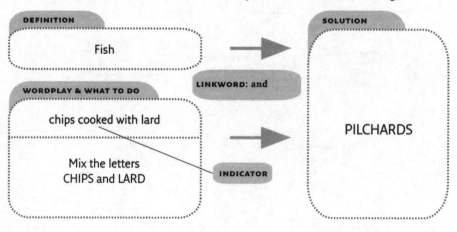

The third example has a nicely misleading definition *port authority* and indicator (to be read as *re-presented*):

ANAGRAM CLUE: In Poole he represented a port authority (9)

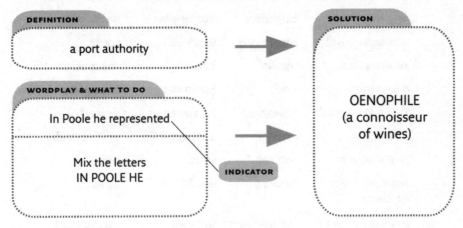

The essential point for indicators of **anagram** clues is that they show a rearrangement, a disturbance to the natural order or a change to be made. There are very many ways of doing this, some reasonably straightforward but others requiring a stretch of the imagination. For example, words and phrases related to drunkenness and madness have to be taken as involving disturbance so that *stoned*, *pickled*, *tight*, *bananas*, *nuts*, *crackers* and *out to lunch* could all be misleading ways to indicate an anagram. I am often asked what are the most common ones but, because there are so many, it is really not possible to reply helpfully. The table that follows is designed to expand on the various categories of rearrangement by giving a few examples of each:

DID YOU KNOW?
Early *Times* crosswords did not indicate an anagram; solvers were required to guess that a mixture of letters was needed but now this is almost universally regarded as unfair on the solver. At present, in some easy puzzles the solver has no doubt about an indicator because a clue may be marked *e.g. Recital (anag.)* for the solution *article*.

INDICATORS FOR ANAGRAM CLUES

ARRANGEMENT	sorted	somehow	anyhow
REARRANGEMENT	revised	reassembled	resort
CHANGE	bursting	out of place	shift
DEVELOPMENT	improved	worked	treat
WRONGNESS	amiss	in error	messed up
STRANGENESS	odd	fantastic	eccentric
DRUNKENNESS	smashed	hammered	lit up
MADNESS	crazy	outraged	up the wall
MOVEMENT	mobile	runs	hit
DISTURBANCE OF ORDER	broken	muddled	upset
INVOLVEMENT	complicated	tangled	implicated

2. The sandwich clue

A sandwich can be considered as bread outside some filling. Similarly in this clue type, the solution can be built from one part(s) being either put **outside** another part or being put **inside** another part.

This is an example of **outside** (with the **indicator** *bottles* being used in its sense of *encloses*):

SANDWICH CLUE: Fan smashing bottles left (9)

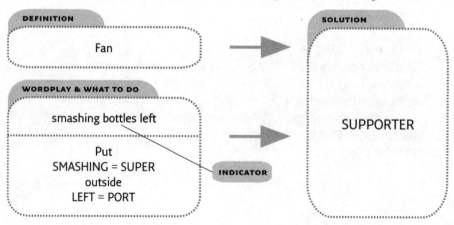

DEFINITION

Fan

WORDPLAY & WHAT TO DO

smashing bottles left

Put
SMASHING = SUPER
outside
LEFT = PORT

INDICATOR

SOLUTION

SUPPORTER

This is an example of **inside**:

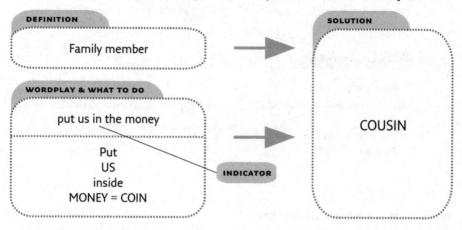

SANDWICH CLUE: Family member put us in the money (6)

DEFINITION

Family member

WORDPLAY & WHAT TO DO

put us in the money

Put
US
inside
MONEY = COIN

INDICATOR

SOLUTION

COUSIN

SOME INDICATORS FOR SANDWICH CLUES

OUTSIDE		
contains	clothing	boxing
houses	harbours	carries
grasping	enclosing	including
restrains	protecting	about

INSIDE		
breaks	cuts	boring
piercing	penetrating	fills
enters	interrupting	amidst
held by	occupies	splitting

Note that *about* has multiple uses in crosswords (see Chapter 10).

3. The homophone clue

In this type, the solution sounds like another word given by the wordplay. The clue is often fairly easy to recognize but it is harder to find the two words which sound alike.

HOMOPHONE CLUE: Reportedly makes pots (4)

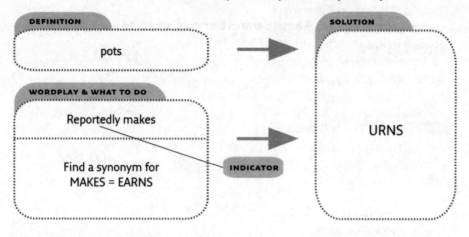

DEFINITION

pots

SOLUTION

URNS

WORDPLAY & WHAT TO DO

Reportedly makes — **INDICATOR**

Find a synonym for
MAKES = EARNS

Indicators for homophone clues:

Anything which gives an impression of sounding like another word such as *so to speak*, *we hear*, *it's said* acts as an indicator. This extends to what's heard in different real-life situations; for example, at home it could be *on the radio*; in the theatre it could be *to an audience*; in the office it could be *for an auditor*.

4. The hidden clue

A **hidden** clue is arguably the easiest type to solve. That's because the letters to be uncovered require no change: they just need to be dug out of the sentence designed to conceal them. In the first example, the indicator is *in*:

HIDDEN CLUE: Parched in the Kalahari desert (4)

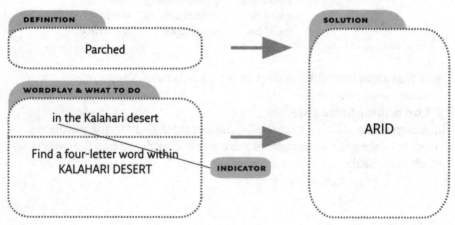

DEFINITION

Parched

SOLUTION

ARID

WORDPLAY & WHAT TO DO

in the Kalahari desert

Find a four-letter word within
KALAHARI DESERT — **INDICATOR**

Indicators for hidden clues:
Commonly *some* (in the sense of a certain part of what follows), *some of*, *partly*, are unique to **hidden** clues; *within, amidst, holding* and *in* can be either **hidden** or **sandwich** indicators.

A variant of the **hidden** clue is where the letters are concealed at intervals within the wordplay, most commonly odd or even letters. You are asked to extract letters that appear as, say, the first, third and fifth letters in the wordplay section of the clue sentence and ignore the intervening letters. Note that there would not normally be superfluous words in such a clue sentence, making it easier to be certain which letters are involved in the extraction.

Here is one such clue in which you have to take only the odd letters of *culture* for the solution.

HIDDEN CLUE: Odd bits of culture such as this (4)

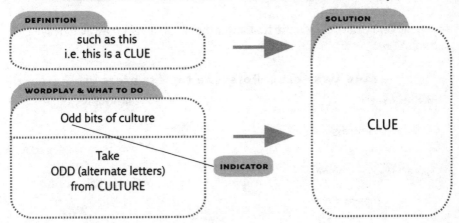

Some indicators for hidden-at-intervals clues:
Oddly, evenly, regularly, ignoring the odds, alternately.

5. The take away clue

A **take away** clue involves something being deducted from something else. This can be one or more letters or a whole word. In the example below it's one letter, *R*, which is an abbreviation of *right* and *get* is an instruction to the solver. It should be noted that abbreviations form an important part of many clue types. You will find in the Appendices a list of those most frequently appearing in *The Times* Crossword.

TAKE AWAY CLUE: Get employed right away in Surrey town (6)

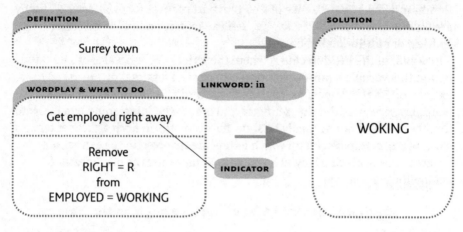

In our second example, it's the first letter that is to be taken away to leave the solution:

TAKE AWAY CLUE: Possess a topless dress (3)

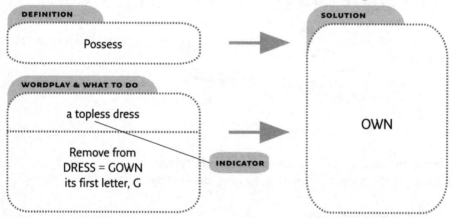

Indicators for take away clues:

These tend to be self-explanatory, such as *reduced*, *less*, *extracted*, but, beware, they can be highly misleading, such as *cast* in a clue concerning the theatre, or *shed* in one ostensibly about the garden. Some indicators inform us that a single letter is to be taken away. These include *short*, *almost*, *nearly* and *most of*, all signifying by long-established convention that the final letter of a word is to be removed. There is more on **take away** indicators such as *unopened*, *disheartened*, *needing no introduction* and *endless* on pages 29-31, which deal with **letter selection** indicators.

6. The reversal clue

The whole of a solution can sometimes be reversed to form another entirely different word. In addition, writing letters backwards or upwards is often part of a clue's wordplay, but for the time being we are concerned with reversal providing the whole of the answer. This is a clue for an across solution:

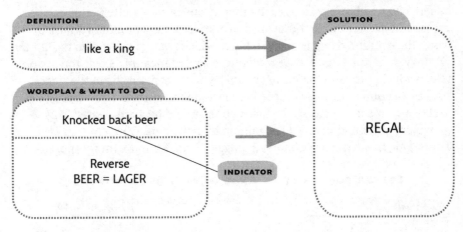

REVERSAL CLUE: Knocked back beer like a king (5)

DEFINITION
like a king

WORDPLAY & WHAT TO DO
Knocked back beer

Reverse
BEER = LAGER

INDICATOR

SOLUTION
REGAL

This is a **reversal** clue for a down solution (see below for an explanation of the difference):

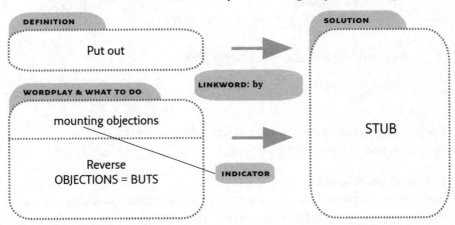

REVERSAL CLUE: Put out by mounting objections (4)

DEFINITION
Put out

LINKWORD: by

WORDPLAY & WHAT TO DO
mounting objections

Reverse
OBJECTIONS = BUTS

INDICATOR

SOLUTION
STUB

Indicators for reversal clues:
Anything showing backward movement, e.g. *around, over, back, recalled.*

It's important to note that some **reversal** indicators apply to **down** clues only, reflecting their position in the grid. The example above of a **down** clue uses *mounting* for this purpose; other possibilities are *up, raised, upset, on the way up, served up*, but be aware that some of these can be used to indicate other types of manipulation, as set out later.

7. The letter switch clue

Where two words differ from each other by one or more letters, this can be exploited by setters so that moving one or more letters produces another word, the solution. Here is an example in which you are instructed to shift the *W* for *West* in *when* in a way that produces a word meaning *axed*. You are not told in which direction the move should be, but it can only be to the right.

An extra point to be brought out here is that if a pause or comma after the first two words is imagined, the instruction should become clearer. This imaginary punctuation effect is common to many crossword clues in *The Times* and elsewhere; see Chapter 4, pages 38-39, for more on this point.

LETTER SWITCH CLUE: Axed when West's moved (4)

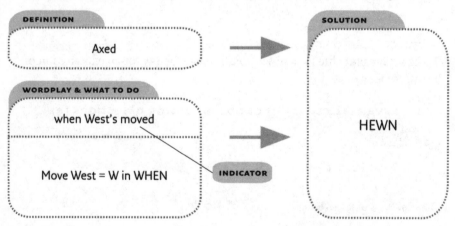

DEFINITION

Axed

SOLUTION

WORDPLAY & WHAT TO DO

when West's moved

HEWN

Move West = W in WHEN

INDICATOR

There is also a form of letter switch in which letters are replaced; see Chapter 8, page 67, for more on this.

8. The all-in-one clue

In the crossword world this is known as **& lit**, christened by Ximenes in the *Observer* series, now in the hands of Azed. However, I have found my workshop participants frequently consider this too cryptic a name! It actually means 'and is literally so' but people tend to puzzle over that at the expense of understanding the concept.

In fact, it is a simple one that I prefer to call **all-in-one**, which is what it is: the definition and wordplay are combined into one, often shortish sentence which, when unscrambled, leads to a description of the solution.

ALL-IN-ONE CLUE: Heads of the several amalgamated Russian states (5)

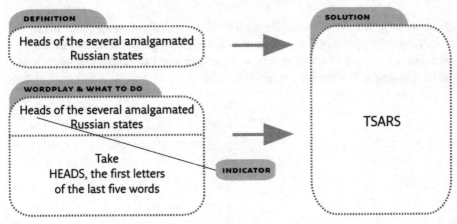

This clue relies on the **letter selection** indicator *heads* (see page 29) to provide the solution. Most of the clueing techniques outlined earlier can be used to make an **all-in-one** clue (see examples in Chapter 8), always providing that the definition and wordplay are one and the same.

Possibly the commonest type is an **all-in-one anagram**, with an anagram as part or all of the wordplay and no extra definition needed because it has been provided by the wordplay. Here is an example:

ALL-IN-ONE ANAGRAM CLUE: Sort of roll, A–E etc? (9)

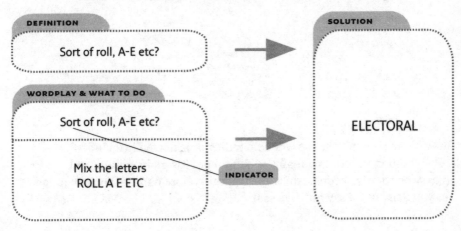

Incidentally, this clue demonstrates how punctuation has to be ignored in clue-solving: the comma and the hyphen play no part in the anagram fodder.

That is not always the case, as explained in Chapter 4 (page 38).

The remaining four types

Now we will focus on the remaining four clue types. Remember that these four normally do not include indicators within the clue sentence. Here they are together in one chart from which we will proceed to examine each one in turn, starting at the top and going clockwise.

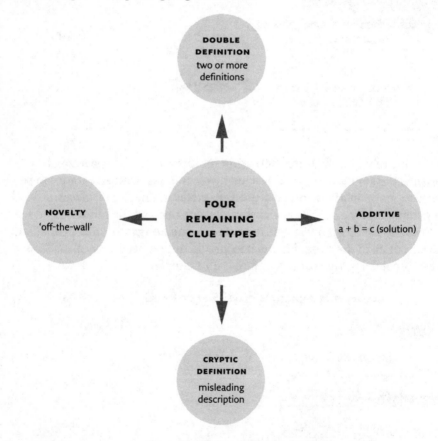

How do we recognize these when no indicator is normally included?

Punctuation may occasionally be helpful but it's mainly intelligent guesswork that's needed. Are these types therefore harder? You can judge for yourself but I'd say not necessarily.

9. The double definition clue

This is simply two, or sometimes more, definitions of the solution side by side. There may be a linking word, as in the second example, such as *is* or *'s*, but most frequently there is none, as in this clue.

DOUBLE DEFINITION CLUE 1: Shoots game (5)

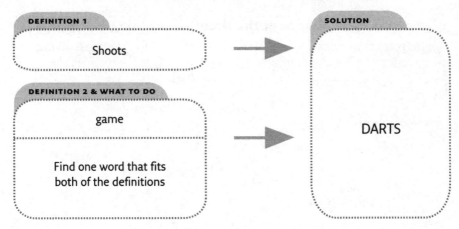

DEFINITION 1

Shoots

DEFINITION 2 & WHAT TO DO

game

Find one word that fits
both of the definitions

SOLUTION

DARTS

DOUBLE DEFINITION CLUE 2: Pools entries making one a rich man (5)

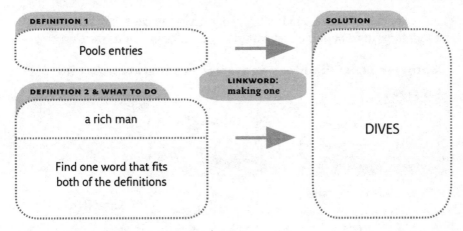

DEFINITION 1

Pools entries

LINKWORD:
making one

DEFINITION 2 & WHAT TO DO

a rich man

Find one word that fits
both of the definitions

SOLUTION

DIVES

Indicators for double definition clues:

No specific indicator is given. It can nonetheless often be guessed by its shortness, or by two or more words, which lack an obvious linkword, or any other obvious indicator. If there are only two words in the clue, it's a very good chance that it's a **double definition**.

10. The additive clue

As we saw at the very beginning of this book, an **additive** clue consists of the solution word being split into parts to form the solution. Sometimes known as a **charade** (from the game of charades, rather than its more modern meaning of 'absurd pretence'), it may perhaps be more helpful to describe it as a simple algebraic expression A + B = solution C. Here is one:

ADDITIVE CLUE: Glance at the fixtures – nothing much on (8)

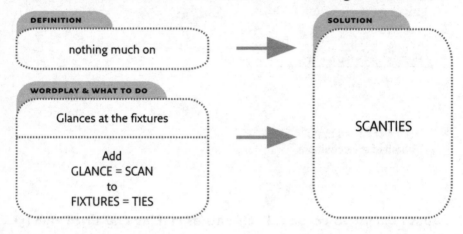

This is another example, made slightly harder by the need to put the second part (*granny*) in front of the first part (*flat*) – as indicated by *as starter*.

ADDITIVE CLUE: Plain nan as starter in separate quarters (6,4)

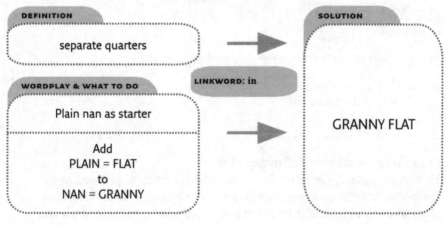

Indicators for additive clues:

With no specific indicator, it's a question rather of spotting that A + B can give C, the solution. Sometimes this is made easier by linkwords such as *facing*, *alongside*, *with*, *next*, indicating that the parts A and B have to be set alongside each other. In the case of **down** clues, the corresponding linkwords would be *on top of*, *looking down on* and similar expressions reflecting the grid position.

11. The cryptic definition clue

There are no component parts at all to this clue, which consists simply of a misleading, usually one-dimensional, way to describe the solution. Depending on how much information is imparted by the clue, it can be very easy or very tough. The best of these clues have an amusing or whimsical air, as in both these examples:

CRYPTIC DEFINITION CLUE 1: Part of Madeira one might sail through (5,2,4)

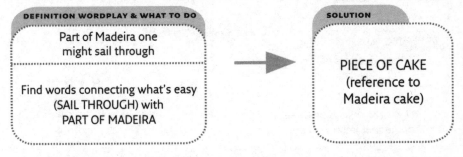

CRYPTIC DEFINITION CLUE 2: Roman marbles lost (3,6,6)

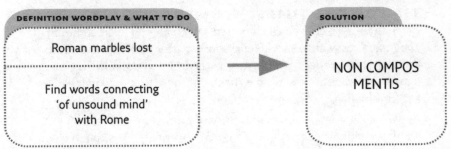

Indicators for cryptic definitions:

The nature of this clue type is such that no indicator is ever given. It can be identified either from the fact that nothing in the clue looks like an indicator, and/or from the presence of a question mark.

12. The novelty clue

Ever since *The Times* Crossword was introduced in 1934, there have been innovative clues conforming to no single pattern which defy categorization into any of the preceding groups. These clues are often solved with extra pleasure.

The setter has found it possible to exploit coincidences or special features of a word. As with the cryptic definition type, the solver is asked to think laterally and throw away any misleading images created by the clue. In some rare circumstances when an especially novel idea is used, there may not even be a proper definition. There are more examples of the **novelty** clue in Chapter 8 but, as a taster, here is one:

NOVELTY CLUE: Eccentric as three-quarters of the characters in Fiji? (5)

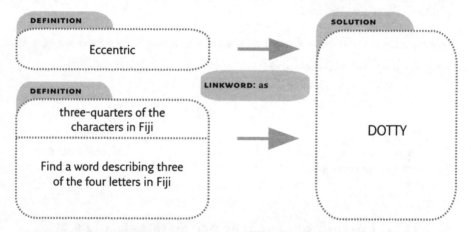

DEFINITION

Eccentric

DEFINITION

three-quarters of the characters in Fiji

Find a word describing three of the four letters in Fiji

LINKWORD: as

SOLUTION

DOTTY

TIP FOR THE TIMES: CLUE FREQUENCY

Given the twelve clue types identified, which are the most common in *The Times* Crossword and will repay closest attention? The answer to this is that frequency patterns vary a little but that the **additive** and **sandwich** types are usually the most common; they may indeed account for half of the total number of clues.

As we shall see later, setters make use of more than one type of wordplay within any one clue so that, for example, a **sandwich** clue can include a **reversal**, a **take away** or an **anagram** element within it. What may help you recognize each clue type is that there is rarely more than one or two of the following types in any one puzzle:

hidden, homophone, all-in-one, novelty, letter switch, double definition, cryptic definition

Letter selection indicators

Before moving on to solving clues, we have to consider how individual letters within clues are signposted. We have seen what sort of indicators go with what sort of clues; now we'll take a look at another commonly used indicator which is essential to solving skills. Take this clue as an example:

ADDITIVE CLUE: Lettuce constituent of salad, primarily (3)

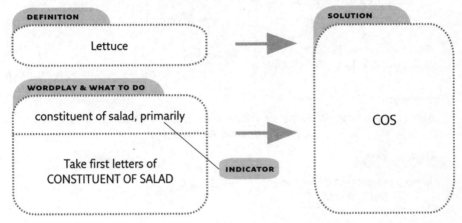

Experienced solvers would be immediately drawn towards the word *primarily* as it indicates that the first letter or (as in this case) letters of the preceding words are to be selected as building blocks to the solution. In more complex clues they could then be subject to further treatment, such as forming part of an anagram, but here they are used simply to form *cos*, the *lettuce* salad ingredient.

There are many alternative ways of showing that the first letter is to be manipulated in some way. Some of these indicators are: *starter, lead, source, opening, top, introduction* and so on. They may be extended to the plural form too with the use of, say, *beginnings, foremost* and *heads*.

Naturally, other positions within words are indicated in a similar fashion. The last letter can be *end, back, finally, tail* and the middle letter *centre, heart*, and all of the inside letters of a word can be *innards, contents, stuffing*.

In their negative **take away** guise, they can be *headless, unopened, failing to start*; and *empty* signifies that the whole of the innards of a word is to be removed.

Overleaf are some examples of letter selection indicators at work:

TAKE AWAY CLUE: Endless industrial action in a Scandinavian port (4)

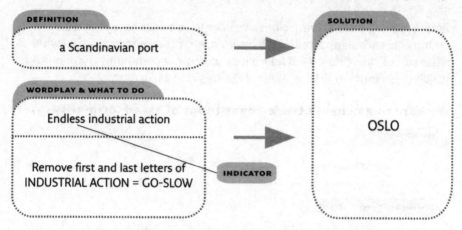

DEFINITION
a Scandinavian port

SOLUTION

WORDPLAY & WHAT TO DO
Endless industrial action

Remove first and last letters of
INDUSTRIAL ACTION = GO-SLOW

INDICATOR

OSLO

ADDITIVE CLUE: What's tedious and instils such listlessness? Every second of this (5)

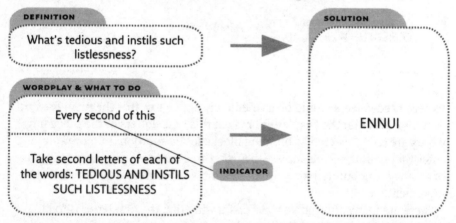

DEFINITION
What's tedious and instils such listlessness?

SOLUTION

WORDPLAY & WHAT TO DO
Every second of this

Take second letters of each of the words: TEDIOUS AND INSTILS SUCH LISTLESSNESS

INDICATOR

ENNUI

After a time, you will become familiar with looking beyond and through the surface meaning of a word doing duty as an indicator so that you realize what you are required to do to the relevant letter(s) or word(s).

Beware **letter selection** indicators that can do double or more duty:

Endless: take away last letter only, or first and last letters
Head: first letter, or take away first letter (in its sense of behead)
Over: sandwich and reversal
Around: sandwich and reversal

Cut: last letter take away, sandwich, anagram
Back: reversal, last letter
Upset: reversal, anagram

Note that in the example below *extremely* indicates first and last letters, not the last letter as is the practice in crosswords such as the Mephisto.

ADDITIVE CLUE: Robin's slayer uses extremely sharp weapon (7)

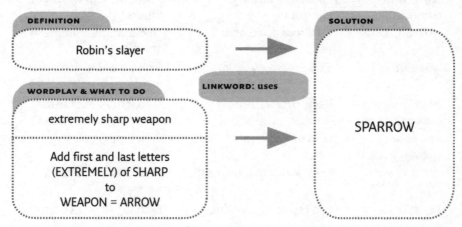

There are examples of indicators throughout this book but it would take an impossibly large volume to include all those used in *The Times*. There are books which list more (as covered in Chapter 15) but even they are not comprehensive. The point to bear in mind is that once you are aware of the possible clue types, you will often be able to infer from a word or words what you are being instructed to do.

What can be difficult, however, is where the same common word in the English language serves as an indicator for several clue types. The words *in* and *about* are the most problematic examples of this and you will find more about these and equally troublesome words in Chapter 10.

Chapters 1–3: summary

Here are two charts offering in summary form the basic points of Chapters 1, 2 and 3. First, a summary of clue types, typical indicators and what the solver must do:

CLUE TYPES	TYPICAL INDICATORS	WHAT TO DO
Types 1–8	**Indicators included in clue**	
ANAGRAM	New, mixed, changing, drunk, in error	Change letters to another word
SANDWICH (OUTSIDE)	Holding, keeps, contains	Put some letters outside others
SANDWICH (INSIDE)	In, breaks, cutting, interrupts	Put some letters inside others
HOMOPHONE	Mentioned, we hear	Find a word sounding like another
HIDDEN	Some, partly, within	Find a word within other words
REVERSAL (ACROSS CLUE)	Back, over, returns	Turn letters backwards
REVERSAL (DOWN CLUE)	Up, over, served up	Turn letters upwards
TAKE AWAY	Less, without, drop, cast	Deduct some letter(s) from a word
LETTER SWITCH	For, replacing, moving	Exchange or move letters
ALL-IN-ONE	Various, depending on wordplay	Use wordplay to find solution which is then defined by the wordplay
Types 9–12	**Indicators (usually) not included in clue**	
ADDITIVE	Usually none given	Add letter(s) to other letter(s)
DOUBLE DEfiNITION	None given	Find solution from two or more distinct definitions, side by side
CRYPTIC DEFINITION	None given	Find solution from puns, hints, ambiguities; ignore surface reading
NOVELTY	None given	Think laterally

Second, let's see how each clue type (apart from a novelty clue) could be applied, using the same solution word in each. That word is *time*, which is defined as *magazine* in all but one clue. The indicators are in bold in each clue.

CLUE TYPES	CLUES FOR THE WORD 'TIME'	WHAT TO DO
Types 1–8		
ANAGRAM	**New** item in magazine	Change letters of ITEM
SANDWICH (OUTSIDE)	Match **bringing in** millions	Put MATCH = TIE outside MILLIONS = M
SANDWICH (INSIDE)	Millions **put into** match magazine	Put MILLIONS = M inside MATCH = TIE
HOMOPHONE	Herb **mentioned** in magazine	Find a word for a HERB sounding like TIME (THYME)
HIDDEN	**Some** sentimental magazine	Find a word within SENTIMENTAL
REVERSAL (ACROSS CLUE)	Magazine issue **backed**	Reverse ISSUE = EMIT
REVERSAL (DOWN CLUE)	Magazine issue **taken up**	Reverse ISSUE = EMIT
TAKE AWAY	**Nameless** chaps behind note in magazine	Remove NAME = N from MEN and add (musical) NOTE = TI
LETTER SWITCH	Magazine volume, one **for** nothing	Replace NOTHING = O in VOLUME = TOME with I
ALL-IN-ONE	Male **interned in** Windsor is doing this?	Put MALE = M inside WINDSOR = TIE (time served by person interned)
Types 9–12 (except novelty clue)		
ADDITIVE	Note yours truly in magazine	Add NOTE = TI to YOURS TRULY = ME
DOUBLE DEFINITION	Bird magazine	Two ways of expressing time, BIRD is time in prison
CRYPTIC DEFINITION	Wilde did it in a sentence	Oscar W in prison

4: Tips for Solving Clues

'Just as in solving a crossword clue, I seem to undergo a quantum leap from the "Haven't the foggiest" state to the "Of course! It's obvious!" state of enlightenment.' Sue Birchmore in *New Scientist*

Having considered clue types and various points associated with each, we will now consider some tips on how you might go about solving them.

Seasoned solvers have many ways of uncovering a clue's solution. What follows are some of these from my own toolkit and the others I have been given for this book. They are in no particular recommended order of importance, except that the first two are often quoted as a way to get started.

1. Find the definition
As you know by now, the definition part of nearly all clues is either at the beginning or end of a clue. Identifying it quickly, and assessing the definition in conjunction with word-length shown, allows the possibility of a good initial guess which can then be checked against wordplay before entry.

2. Find an indicator and/or clue type
Not all clues have indicators, as we have seen, but where they do, try to use them to identify the clue type. For example, you may spot a familiar anagram indicator such as *drunk* or *battered* and thence compare the letters in the **anagram fodder** with the word-length of the solution given. If they correspond, there is a good chance that you have identified the wordplay element of the clue and can develop that into a possible solution.

3. Ignore the scenario
A setter for *The Times* Crossword does his or her best to produce clues which paint believable, realistic pictures. After quickly admiring the effort made, I suggest that it's best to ignore it totally and look at the individual components in front of you. Take the clue overleaf about a cricket bowler:

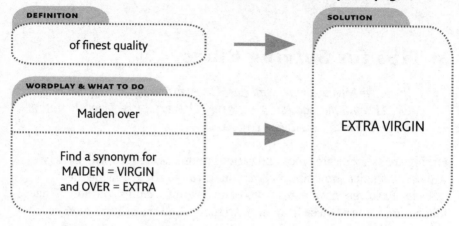

You can be pretty sure that thinking for too long about a top-class bowler on a lovely summer's day at Lord's will not be productive. Thinking of your pantry and cooking may be more useful as it's a **double definition** in which a *maiden over* or surplus is an *extra virgin*.

4. Exploit word-lengths
Use friendly word-lengths such as 4,2,3,4 with the central two being perhaps something of a gift like *in the* or *of the*; and 4,4,1,4 nearly always embracing the letter A, from which something like *once upon a time* may be the answer.

5. Study every word
Consider each word carefully, separately and together. Disregard phrases which go naturally together such as, say, *silver wedding*, and split them into their parts. It could be that the definition is *silver* on its own.

In doing this, think of all the meanings of a word rather than the one that comes first into your head.

For example, forget *drink* in its marine sense and switch to *alcohol*. The indicator *some* reveals a **hidden** clue and *medoc* pops out.

HIDDEN CLUE: Some termed ocean the drink (5)

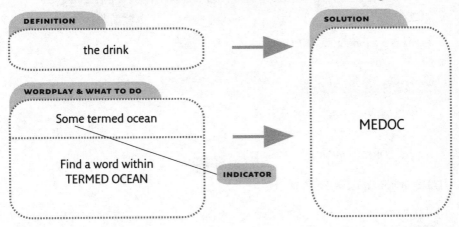

Here is another misleading image in the second example below, which has nothing to do with DIY:

ADDITIVE CLUE INCLUDING ANAGRAM: Having broken desk, go off to get bolt (9)

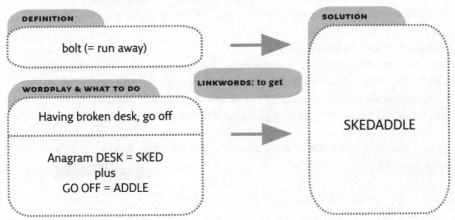

Last, an instance, overleaf, of how separating the sentence into even its smallest parts is sometimes needed. This clue also demonstrates the use of a **letter selection** indicator for the final two letters (as seen in Chapter 3, page 29).

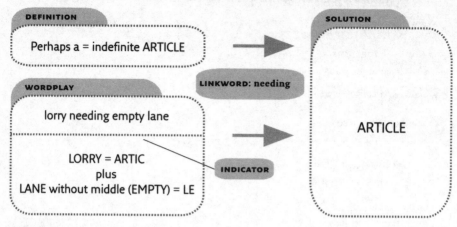

ADDITIVE CLUE: Perhaps a lorry needing empty lane (7)

DEFINITION

Perhaps a = indefinite ARTICLE

WORDPLAY

lorry needing empty lane

LORRY = ARTIC
plus
LANE without middle (EMPTY) = LE

LINKWORD: needing

INDICATOR

SOLUTION

ARTICLE

6. Write bars in grid

Given word-lengths that indicate more than one complete word (e.g. 3-7, or 3,7), some solvers automatically write the word divisions as bar-lines into the grid and find that helps. The bars can be either vertical or horizontal depending on whether they are split words or hyphenated words. This little trick can be especially useful when the word to be found is in two parts and the first letter, say, of the second of the parts is given by an intersecting solution.

7. Ignore punctuation

In a nutshell, only exclamation marks and question marks are meaningful in clues; other punctuation should usually be ignored. For example, the **anagram fodder** can include letters or words with a comma or other punctuation in between, as in this clue seen earlier:

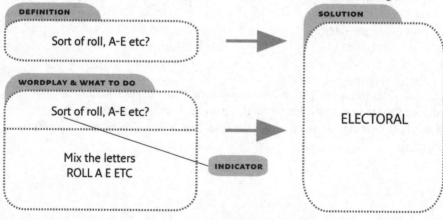

ALL-IN-ONE ANAGRAM CLUE: Sort of roll, A-E etc? (9)

DEFINITION

Sort of roll, A-E etc?

WORDPLAY & WHAT TO DO

Sort of roll, A-E etc?

Mix the letters
ROLL A E ETC

INDICATOR

SOLUTION

ELECTORAL

Another example of this is seen in the **hidden** clue that follows:

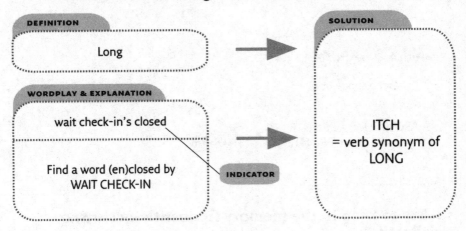

SANDWICH CLUE: Long wait – check-in's closed (4)

DEFINITION

Long

WORDPLAY & EXPLANATION

wait check-in's closed

Find a word (en)closed by
WAIT CHECK-IN

INDICATOR

SOLUTION

ITCH
= verb synonym of
LONG

There is more on punctuation in Chapter 9.

8. Guess

An inspired guess can work wonders. You just feel that you know the answer without recognizing why. I have watched this process in my workshops and it's a magical, intuitive process. On one occasion a lady in her late 80s was often able to come up with the answers but had no idea how she had done so. However, this method works for only a few people and, even then, only for a few clues and it does have the danger of ending up with the wrong solution in the grid.

9. Think commas

One of the most useful tips I received as a novice was to imagine a comma in any part of the clue sentence. As we have seen in nearly all the examples so far, clues consist frequently of a string of words, each one of which has a part to play, and separating them into their meaningful parts can prove very helpful. In this clue overleaf, imagining a pause between the last two words makes the solution much easier:

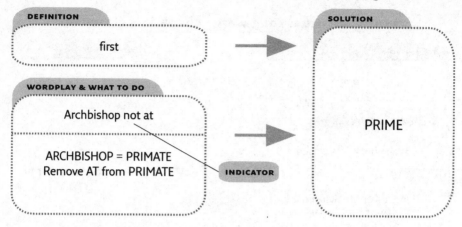

TAKE AWAY CLUE: Archbishop? Not at first (5)

DEFINITION

first

SOLUTION

WORDPLAY & WHAT TO DO

Archbishop not at

ARCHBISHOP = PRIMATE
Remove AT from PRIMATE

INDICATOR

PRIME

10. Try to keep in the memory frequently-occurring small words

As you come across them, store up words like *pig*, *sow*, *cow*, *tup* and *hog* for *farm animal* (or even just *animal*) and try these first.

11. Advice on cracking anagrams

Let us assume that you have identified an **anagram** indicator, counted the number of letters in the **anagram fodder**, including any abbreviations, and seen that they make up the given word-length. What techniques are there to find the solution?

People have their own familiar way of sorting out anagrams. The simplest method involves finding the right combination from careful scrutiny of the letters, looking for the commonly occurring *-ing*, *-tion*, *-er*, *-or* endings.

If this does not work, the anagram fodder can then be written down in various ways: in a straight line, in a diamond shape, in a circle or in random order. With longer anagrams, this can involve several rewrites in different orders until the answer emerges.

In cases where the definition is something not very specific, such as *plant* or *animal*, it may be best to defer resolution until some intersecting letters have been entered.

Finally there are of course electronic aids as listed in Chapter 15 which can take all the pain (but also maybe some of the enjoyment) out of the process.

5: Tips for Solving the Whole Puzzle

'This clue once found, unravels all the rest.' Alexander Pope, 'Epistle to Lord Cobham'

Now let's consider some points for tackling the whole of a puzzle.

1. Write in pencil or ink?

I'm not sure it matters much as long as you avoid inking in firmly before you have worked out both the definition and wordplay. There is nothing worse than being held up for a long time by an incorrect entry made in haste. A thoughtful Christmas present bought for me some years ago was the delightful compromise of a pen with ink that could be erased – it still works well.

2. Empty grid: how to start?

You have a puzzle in front of you which looks totally impossible – maybe you begin to feel inadequate. Forget that; most puzzles, by accident or design, give you at least one clue to get you going and all you have to do is find it! It may be a **hidden** clue; after all, the letters of the solution are there facing you as part of the clue. So scan the clues for an indicator.

But supposing the mean setter has not included a **hidden** clue today. What should you do when there appears to be no way in? There are various points:

- It is rare for there to be no **anagram** clue in *The Times* Crossword, so why not scan for an **anagram** indicator? Once found, the letters are there as with **hidden** clues, waiting to be unscrambled.
- Try to spot an obvious definition. One experienced solver told me he can see a definition nearly always instantly – but that was after 40 years of solving!
- At this stage it's a good idea to find a clue that seems to be within your areas of interests or expertise. For example, in my case it is always comforting to spot clues which have a musical, political or a sporting component. Of course I take into account that I may be being led up the garden path.

- Look for short solutions of up to five letters because there are fewer words that can fit the space indicated. While it's rewarding to get the 15-letter word at 1 across immediately, that is rare.
- Try the compound phrases that are present in most puzzles. As covered earlier, the likes of 3,2,4 and 4,4,1,4 are a gift in the sense that the shorter lengths can often be guessed.
- Keep in mind that the tense of the clue and the solution must be the same. So look for plurals, -*ing* and -*ed* in potential definitions. Try to formulate an answer from this but beware inking in such endings in error.
- Look in the clues for unusual words and proper names and ask yourself why they may have been included. Getting into the setter's mind in this respect and in other aspects of cryptic clues can be rewarding.

START AT THE BOTTOM RIGHT HAND CORNER?

More than one solver I know, and champion solver John Sykes (see Chapter 13), consider that you should look here first as the setter, having written the clues in order from 1 across, is tired by the time the bottom of the grid is reached. Hence the clues are easier than elsewhere. Based on my own setting pattern, I'm sceptical about this but, nonetheless, if that approach helps you to gain the confidence essential to solving, I'd say stick with it.

3. How to continue?

After one clue is solved, where next? This advice may be very helpful: build on the most promising (i.e. unusual) of the intersecting letters you have available. Don't attempt clues for which you have no letters until you become convinced you can make no progress with the letters you have. Crossword solving is a process of gains being built up cumulatively and, at this early stage, there may or may not be gains to make.

Try a little harder to crack clues that yield the best follow-on letters, e.g. those running across the top and down the sides. As one of my correspondents said, first letters are worth a lot. Also when more letters are available, you may find that you can anticipate solutions from letter patterns such as -*ation*, -*ive*, -*ally* and the like.

TIP FOR THE TIMES: DAY BY DAY

It is often thought that puzzles on Monday are the easiest of the week (as people have less time) and get harder during the week. While this may be so for other newspapers it is not the case for *The Times*. Nor are there fixed days for setters as happens elsewhere; setters' puzzles are mixed about to keep solvers guessing.

6. The Knowledge

> 'In conclusion, may I commend your public spirit in putting the good old Emu back into circulation as you did a few days ago? We of the canaille know that the Sun-God Ra has apparently retired from active work (and) are immensely grateful for the occasional Emu.' P.G. Wodehouse, 1934 letter to *The Times*

Some items which are common to many puzzles and which, after a time, you will take for granted are covered in this next chapter. Just as it takes London cabbies some years to acquire all the information needed for their task, so it is with crosswords. What follows is a randomly ordered set of items that I hope helps you along the way to becoming a *Times* Crossword solver of excellence.

1. Numerals
Numerals, chiefly **roman**, are common so in alphabetical order you will find:

eleven	xi	hundred	c
fifty	l	nine	ix
five	v	six	vi
five hundred	d	ten	x
four	iv	thousand	m and k

Numbers such as eighteen (XVIII) are unlikely to be met for obvious reasons.

2. Compass points
Equally common are compass points. The abbreviations for north, south, east and west and their two-letter combinations need no listing here but beware *point* or *quarter* which can do duty for any of the four. This can involve testing each in turn to see whether it yields part of, or the full, solution. Occasionally you may need to think of three-letter compass points, as in this clue:

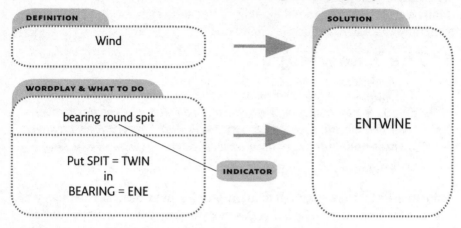

SANDWICH CLUE: Wind bearing round spit (7)

DEFINITION
Wind

SOLUTION

WORDPLAY & WHAT TO DO
bearing round spit

Put SPIT = TWIN
in
BEARING = ENE

INDICATOR

ENTWINE

Naturally, N,E,W and S are Bridge players too (see page 49).

3. Foreign languages

Some knowledge of foreign languages is needed but only of simple words in the more familiar, usually European, languages. Thus German articles *der*, *die* or *das*; French ones *le*, *la* or *l'*; and Spanish *el*, *la* or *los*; and the equivalent indefinite articles in these languages are regarded as fair game as are common French words such as *oui*, *rue* and *et*. Look out for misleading indications of Frenchness such as *Nice*, *Angers* and *Nancy*. Here's a more straightforward example:

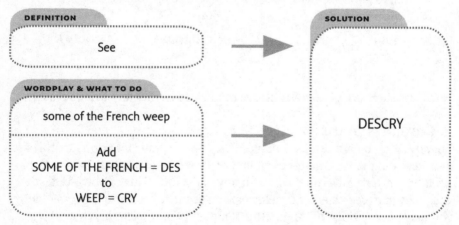

ADDITIVE CLUE: See some of the French weep (6)

DEFINITION
See

SOLUTION

WORDPLAY & WHAT TO DO
some of the French weep

Add
SOME OF THE FRENCH = DES
to
WEEP = CRY

DESCRY

4. Military types

Military types can appear in their abbreviated form as below but also more generally as soldier(s), officer(s), rank, unit(s) and the like.

American soldier	GI	gunners	RA
artillery	RA	lieutenant	LT
colonel	COL	officer	NCO, OC
engineers	RE	other ranks	OR
general	GEN		

5. Rivers

Rivers feature in crosswords as the abbreviation *R* and also, because of their size, the *Po*, *Exe* or *Dee*. As always it's trial and error that unlocks which particular one is required. Another more esoteric expression of *river* is *flower* (see Chapter 10, page 102).

6. Alphabets

A brief recall of some alphabets may come in handy. In particular:

- **Greek letters**: beta, chi, delta, eta, iota, phi, pi, psi.
- **Nato**: alpha, bravo, Charlie, delta, echo, foxtrot, golf, hotel, India, Juliet, kilo, lima, Mike, November, Oscar, papa, Quebec, Romeo, sierra, tango, uniform, victor, whiskey, X-ray, Yankee, Zulu.

7. Cricket terms

Though many sports and games do appear in crosswords (golf perhaps more than soccer or rugby), the quaint (often short) terms and frequent abbreviations used in cricket are a gift to setters. Female solvers, especially participants on my workshops, tell me this is a cause of frustration, so here are the cricket abbreviations likely to be encountered:

In addition, these cricket terms are not unknown in *The Times* Crossword: batting (IN), extra (BYE), leg (ON), ton (C – one hundred) and deliveries (OVER).

bowled	B	maiden	M
bye	B	one-day international	ODI
caught	C or CT	run or runs	R
duck	O	run out	RO
eleven	XI	stumped	ST
fifty	L	wicket	W
hundred	C	wide	W
length	L		

8. Chemical elements

Remember your chemical elements? Here are those most beloved of setters:

arsenic	AS	iron	FE
copper	CU	silver	AG
gold	AU or OR	tungsten	W

The following wonderfully misleading effort uses another:

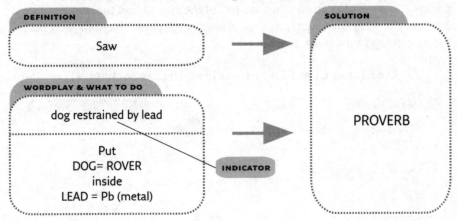

SANDWICH CLUE: Saw dog restrained by lead (7)

DEFINITION: Saw

WORDPLAY & WHAT TO DO: dog restrained by lead

Put
DOG= ROVER
inside
LEAD = Pb (metal)

INDICATOR

SOLUTION: PROVERB

9. The City of London

Though now effectively split across several postal areas including Canary Wharf, in crosswords it is still thought of as the old Square Mile; actually not even all of it (EC2), just EC for City or The City in wordplay, as below in a clue with a debatable sentiment:

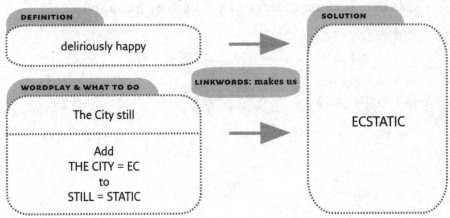

ADDITIVE CLUE: The City still makes us deliriously happy (8)

DEFINITION: deliriously happy

WORDPLAY & WHAT TO DO: The City still

Add
THE CITY = EC
to
STILL = STATIC

LINKWORDS: makes us

SOLUTION: ECSTATIC

10. Chess

Chess notations that appear are: bishop (B), king (K), knight (N), pawn (P), queen (Q), rook (R).

11. Names

In part of the wordplay, names of boys and girls can be indicated by the terse *boy* or *girl*, etc. Maybe *Ed*, *Ted* and *Ian* are the most common but the best advice is to work back from other aspects of the clue to find the name in question. In this rather hard clue, you would need to find the definition first before coming to the particular lad:

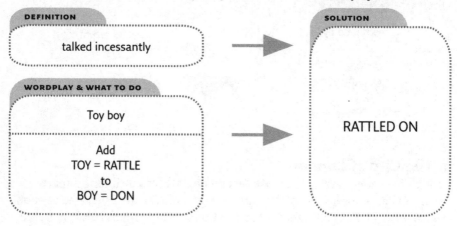

ADDITIVE CLUE: Toy boy talked incessantly (7,2)

DEFINITION	SOLUTION
talked incessantly	
WORDPLAY & WHAT TO DO	RATTLED ON
Toy boy	
Add TOY = RATTLE to BOY = DON	

... and here's a less common name in an enjoyable clue:

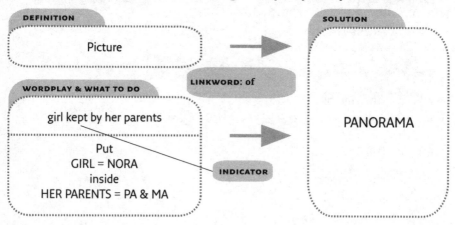

SANDWICH CLUE: Picture of girl kept by her parents (8)

DEFINITION	SOLUTION
Picture	
LINKWORD: of	
WORDPLAY & WHAT TO DO	PANORAMA
girl kept by her parents	
Put GIRL = NORA inside HER PARENTS = PA & MA **INDICATOR**	

12. Setters

Despite the fact that *Times* Crossword setters remain anonymous, he or she does appear in clues. This can be as *Yours Truly*, *I* or *me* within wordplay. Here's an example:

SANDWICH CLUE: Rather restricting the setter? I don't care! (8)

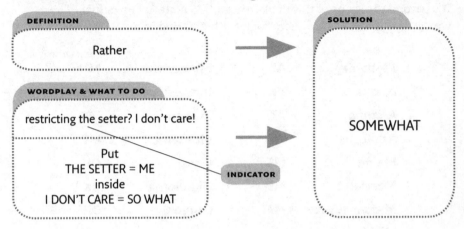

DEFINITION

Rather

WORDPLAY & WHAT TO DO

restricting the setter? I don't care!

Put
THE SETTER = ME
inside
I DON'T CARE = SO WHAT

INDICATOR

SOLUTION

SOMEWHAT

13. Bridge

Bridge notation can feature in terms of north, south, east and west in abbreviated form; and this can extend to Bridge partners or as here:

ADDITIVE CLUE: Heart led by opponents at bridge – play again! (6)

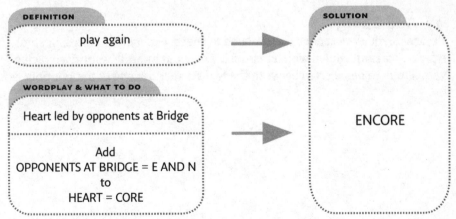

DEFINITION

play again

WORDPLAY & WHAT TO DO

Heart led by opponents at Bridge

Add
OPPONENTS AT BRIDGE = E AND N
to
HEART = CORE

SOLUTION

ENCORE

14. Accents and other punctuation

Accents, hyphens and apostrophes are of course included in clue sentences but, by convention, they are not entered into the grid. For example, *its* and *it's* in clues would be entered in the same way (as the former) in the grid.

15. Some US states

It's beyond the scope of this book to list all US state abbreviations. Those which appear more than others begin with A, O and M:

Alabama	AL	Minnesota	MN
Alaska	AK	Mississippi	MS
Arizona	AZ	Missouri	MO
Arkansas	AR	Montana	MT
Maine	ME	Ohio	OH
Maryland	MD	Oklahoma	OK
Massachusetts	MA	Oregon	OR
Michigan	MI		

16. Workers

The word *worker* could be a reference to the human kind but, more likely, it will be a synonym for *ant* or *bee*.

17. And finally...

Phrases such as *on board* can be related to chess, e.g. men or pieces, or ships, e.g. SS (= steam ship) in which case *on board* could indicate a **sandwich** clue with letters to be inserted between the two s's at either end of the solution.

7. Ten Things to Consider When Stuck

'One came to me in the night.' Fiona Macleod, *A Song of Dreams*

Even the best solvers get held up or seriously stuck at times. Here are ten reasons why you may also draw a blank, with suggestions of how to make a breakthrough.

1. Check for a wrong entry

The first point to consider is whether you have made a mistake in an earlier entry. Once a word is 'inked' into the grid, you naturally become reluctant to consider other possibilities for the solution in question.

Even experienced hands trip up by inserting incorrect answers into the grid too quickly, for example without having matched wordplay to definition or vice versa. It's maddening to spend a long time working from wrong assumptions so do check this possibility first.

2. Ignore the surface reading

The vital fact to keep in mind is that the setter's aim is to produce a sentence that appears to mean one thing but may well, and usually does, mean something totally different. In the very best clues, this is achieved by the creation of a highly misleading image. The solver's response is to enjoy the image but ignore it – the solution may come out after a close examination of each word rather than appreciation of the scenario presented. Try not to miss the subtlety of a clue, but only after being sure of the solution.

3. Look carefully again and consider each word in the clue

Cunning setters find ways of using familiar combinations and juxtapositions which require splitting before any progress can be made. Consider the clue below.

You may well get stuck on this until you realize that the two words *British Isles* need to be separated to uncover the definition.

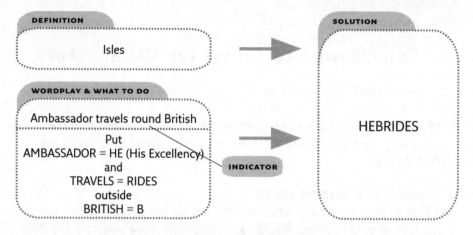

SANDWICH CLUE: Ambassador travels round British Isles (8)

DEFINITION

Isles

WORDPLAY & WHAT TO DO

Ambassador travels round British

Put
AMBASSADOR = HE (His Excellency)
and
TRAVELS = RIDES
outside
BRITISH = B

INDICATOR

SOLUTION

HEBRIDES

TIP FOR THE TIMES
Use of misleading parts of speech is a strong feature of *The Times* Crossword, setting it apart from easier crosswords. Participants in my workshops are misled time and again by this and my suggestion is that, when temporarily stuck, you reconsider carefully every word of the clue which could have an alternative part of speech.

4. Endings

Based on a definition in the past tense, you may have pencilled or, even worse, inked in the ending *-ed* when the actual solution is, say, *caught* or *known*. Similar problems can arise after putting in an *-s* or an *-ing* – sensible practice, usually, but needing reconsideration when you are stuck.

5. Take a break to do something else

This is the most popular tip of all from experienced solvers. Doing the washing up or taking the dog for a walk has the most liberating effect on the blocked crossword mind. You may find that this extends to finding a solution the next morning – or even during the night.

6. Ring the help line

If you cannot wait that long, the solution to the current day's puzzle can be obtained via a phone call to the number shown at the foot of each day's puzzle.

7. 'Cheat' via electronic aids and the internet

Crosswords are an entertainment and you make your own rules as regards using electronic aids. Using dictionaries to confirm a solution is just common sense; going further to root out a solution is now much easier than dictionary-bashing as electronic aids and the internet virtually guarantee finding tricky answers.

Is this cheating? Typically half the audience at one of my talks will be firmly against what they see as cheating; the other half see it differently as a means of doing more puzzles per day. I suppose the ultimate, if that's what you want, is the Crossword Maestro program. It reckons to solve a high percentage of *Times* clues but that surely takes the fun out of the whole process.

Without going that far, and if conventional dictionary/thesaurus hunting has failed or is too time-consuming, you can try a word completion tool. Some of these are listed in Chapter 15.

8. Consult the blog specifically for *The Times* Crossword

See Chapter 15. Not only does this usually give the answer on the day of the publication but it often also gives the wordplay or an explanation.

9. Phone a friend

It's remarkable how two or more brains working on a clue can come up with answers much more effectively than one (as seen in workshops, groups of three or four are often amazingly successful in speeding up solving).

10. Ask the Cluru

If you still need help in understanding why a solution is the answer to what was published, there are services available for this too. One such is for Crossword Club members (also see Chapter 14) offered by the Cluru (Clue Guru, currently myself). It is noticeable with the advent of blogs that requests are fewer than they once were and the resource now primarily helps those who do not use computers. Sometimes queries refer to puzzles from many years ago where someone has seemingly been pondering a crossword conundrum for a very long time. In one instance a query that was answered satisfactorily related to a pre-war puzzle!

PART 2

MASTERING THE TIMES CROSSWORD

8. Finer Points of Clues

'A crossword is an unusual puzzle in that you can derive enjoyment from it, even if you cannot complete it entirely... provided that the setter has shown wit, wisdom and elegance.' Hugh Stephenson, *Secrets of the Setters*

At this point, we move up from basics to outline the finer points of clues and puzzles. In the charts from now on, wordplay analysis is given as an explanation rather than an indication of what to do.

Assuming that you do not wish to go along with the sentiment of the above quotation, we will consider the finer points of the basics with the aim of helping you finish what you have started. We'll start with the finer points associated with clue types, and then those that apply generally to all clues.

1. The anagram clue: finer points

From now on, we will indicate which words form the **anagram fodder** by an asterisk (*).

Anagram fodder: which letters? (1)

Some crosswords require you to find an interim solution and then make an anagram of that. Called an **indirect anagram**, the practice is not used in *The Times*. However, where there is a unique interim solution such as *omicron* (pi's predecessor in the Greek alphabet), you may see a clue such as the one overleaf.

ANAGRAM CLUE 1: It's crazy changing what comes before pi (7)

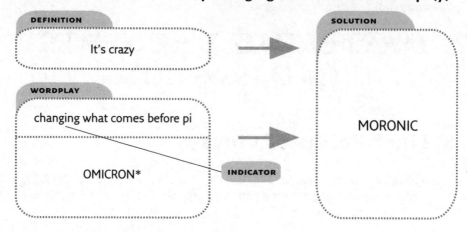

DEFINITION

It's crazy

WORDPLAY

changing what comes before pi

OMICRON*

INDICATOR

SOLUTION

MORONIC

Anagram fodder: which letters? (2)

Some substitution may be needed before the **anagram fodder** is available. Here, an abbreviation *O* for *none* is to be exchanged with *era*, signalled by *ages*.

ANAGRAM CLUE 2 (WITH LETTER SWITCH): Farewell horrid lepidoptera – none seen for ages (6-3)

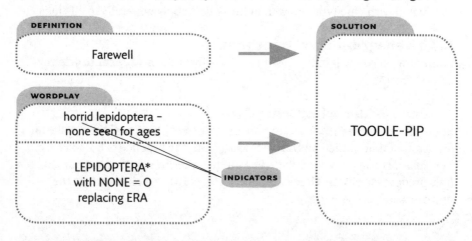

DEFINITION

Farewell

WORDPLAY

horrid lepidoptera – none seen for ages

LEPIDOPTERA*
with NONE = O
replacing ERA

INDICATORS

SOLUTION

TOODLE-PIP

TIP FOR THE TIMES

It is rare for there to be no anagrams in a *Times* puzzle and equally rare to find more than four or five in total, with two-part anagrams counting as one whole-word anagram.

Anagram fodder: which letters? (3)

The **anagram fodder** can be part of a hyphenated word, as here:

ANAGRAM CLUE: Aspiring to achieve first in Wimbledon, double-faulted (5-2)

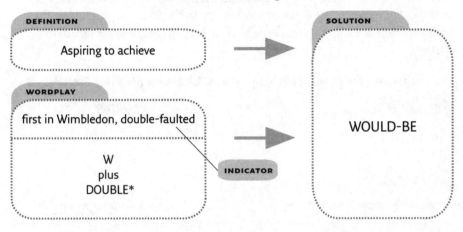

DEFINITION

Aspiring to achieve

WORDPLAY

first in Wimbledon, double-faulted

W
plus
DOUBLE*

INDICATOR

SOLUTION

WOULD-BE

Position of the indicator

While anagrams are always indicated in one of the many ways already covered in Chapter 3, the position of the indicator is not always immediately next to the **anagram fodder**. In the clue below, a letter has to be deducted before the anagram can be unscrambled:

ANAGRAM CLUE: Neglectful having left off dicky bow (9)

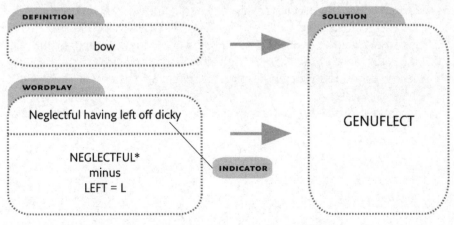

DEFINITION

bow

WORDPLAY

Neglectful having left off dicky

NEGLECTFUL*
minus
LEFT = L

INDICATOR

SOLUTION

GENUFLECT

2. The sandwich clue: finer points

The basis of this clue type, something inside something else, is probably the technique most commonly encountered in *Times* puzzles, so its tricks and quirks should repay study.

Its use in any one clue may be in conjunction with, say, an **anagram**, and be indicated by a less than obvious indicator. In the following example, the indicator *stop* is used in its sense of *block* or *plug* (perhaps more normally *stop up*):

SANDWICH CLUE: Nothing stops Chelsea playing tie (8)

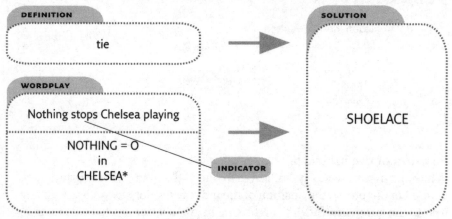

DEFINITION

tie

WORDPLAY

Nothing stops Chelsea playing

NOTHING = O
in
CHELSEA*

INDICATOR

SOLUTION

SHOELACE

CONFUSING 'HIDDEN' AND 'SANDWICH'

I find my workshop participants easily confuse **hidden** and **sandwich** clues, partly because their indicators are similar. The difference is that in **hidden** clues, the word to be found is contained exactly (albeit with intervening punctuation sometimes) within the clue sentence. In **sandwich** clues, the solution word is to be constructed by the solver from the separate elements available.

Sometimes the element to be sandwiched is difficult to disentangle, as in this clue, which we looked at before in another context:

SANDWICH CLUE: Rather restricting the setter? I don't care! (8)

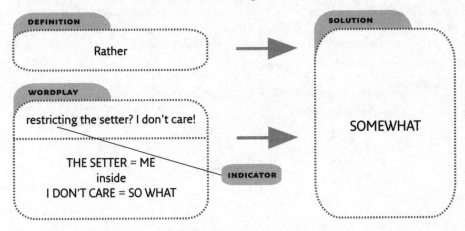

DEFINITION

Rather

WORDPLAY

restricting the setter? I don't care!

THE SETTER = ME
inside
I DON'T CARE = SO WHAT

INDICATOR

SOLUTION

SOMEWHAT

One might initially assume that *I don't care* is the definition when in fact it is part of the wordplay which consists of all the words of the clue except the first word *rather*. As so often, a comma must be imagined between the first and second words before you can solve the clue.

The sandwich can be formed with a kind of reverse construction, as here:

SANDWICH CLUE: Fall in love? On the contrary, wilt (5)

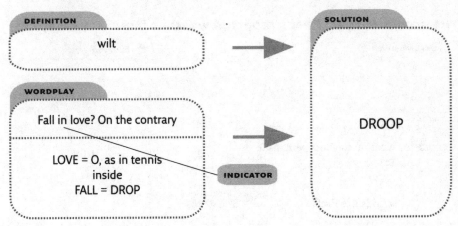

DEFINITION

wilt

WORDPLAY

Fall in love? On the contrary

LOVE = O, as in tennis
inside
FALL = DROP

INDICATOR

SOLUTION

DROOP

Here is a very misleading **sandwich**, boasting an unusual indicator and the word *for* that looks as if it is a linkword but isn't:

SANDWICH CLUE: Composer of lines for Soviet city (8)

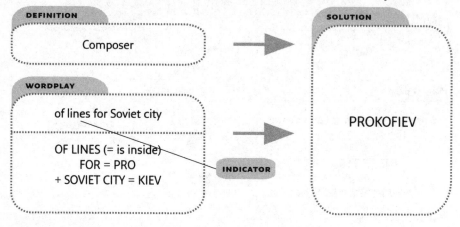

DEFINITION

Composer

WORDPLAY

of lines for Soviet city

OF LINES (= is inside)
FOR = PRO
+ SOVIET CITY = KIEV

INDICATOR

SOLUTION

PROKOFIEV

The message is that study of each word individually is essential.

3. The homophone clue: finer points
In the best clue-writing, you should be left in no doubt in a **homophone** clue as to which word is the solution and which the wordplay. For example, the solution to the next clue could be *rain* or *rein* and the ambiguity would be avoided if the indicator *reported* were moved to the end of the sentence.

HOMOPHONE CLUE: Check reported weather forecast perhaps (4)

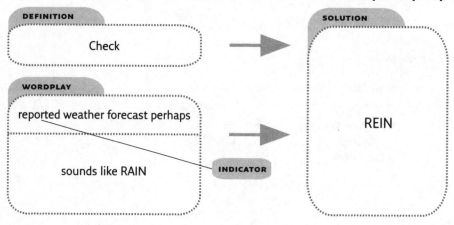

DEFINITION

Check

WORDPLAY

reported weather forecast perhaps

sounds like RAIN

INDICATOR

SOLUTION

REIN

The *Times* Crossword only rarely contains **reverse homophones**; that is to say, the **homophone** is in the clue, rather than the solution. Here's an example of a **reverse homophone**:

HOMOPHONE CLUE: Egg on a steak, say (4)

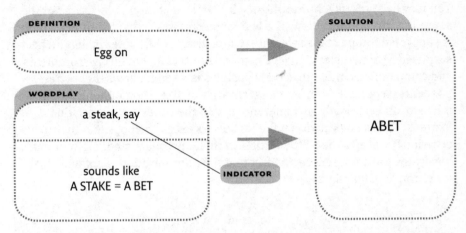

This is another **reverse homophone** which has the attraction of using alphabet letters in a novel way:

HOMOPHONE CLUE: Characters in front of queue, say highly placed (4)

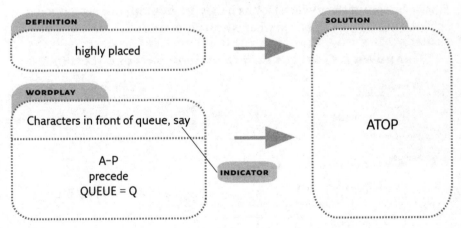

You may be stuck on a **homophone** clue because its sound to you is not the same as your pronunciation. The test for setters is whether the pronunciation is supported by one of the reference dictionaries (see Chapter 15) but I'd be surprised if, nonetheless, *Times* Crossword setters do not receive comments and complaints on this subject. My postbag as a setter shows that correspondents (especially from Scotland) strongly dislike a homophone they do not relate to, and especially so if inference is that the setter's pronunciation is 'correct'. That's not strictly a point for solvers except perhaps that they may occasionally need to be a little flexible in their approach to homophone clues. Ideally the indicator reflects the fact that the pronunciation is not universal: for example, *some may say*.

Finally, beware of clues which look as if they are **homophones** – you could easily be misled here by *said* in what is actually a **sandwich** clue:

SANDWICH CLUE: It's said to include part of circuit (7)

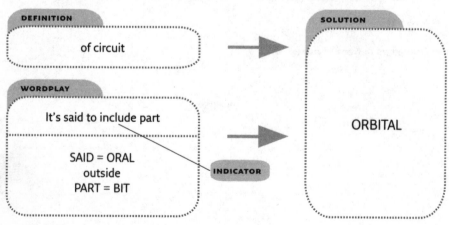

DEFINITION
of circuit

SOLUTION

WORDPLAY
It's said to include part

SAID = ORAL
outside
PART = BIT

INDICATOR

ORBITAL

4. The hidden clue: finer points

The indicator may be at the end of the clue sentence as in the example below, in which the interpretation should be that a synonym of *zip* is being *employed* by the letters that follow it:

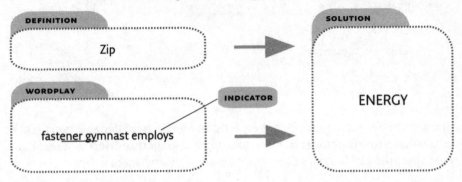

HIDDEN CLUE: Zip fastener gymnast employs (6)

DEFINITION	SOLUTION
Zip	
WORDPLAY	ENERGY
fast*ener gy*mnast employs	

INDICATOR

Also in a more difficult category, the solution can be spread over more than two words:

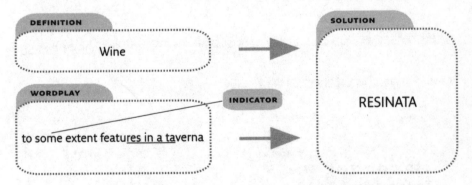

HIDDEN CLUE: Wine to some extent features in a taverna (8)

DEFINITION	SOLUTION
Wine	
WORDPLAY	RESINATA
to some extent featu*res in a ta*verna	

INDICATOR

The letters concealed may have to be reversed before the solution is discovered, as overleaf:

HIDDEN CLUE: Swimmer turning in special pool (6)

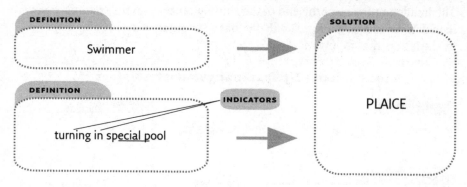

You should be on the lookout for very long and well-concealed solutions. This next wonderful effort must be close to being the longest **hidden** clue that has ever appeared in *The Times* Crossword (or possibly anywhere else):

HIDDEN CLUE: As seen in jab, reach of pro miserably failing to meet expectations (6,2,7)

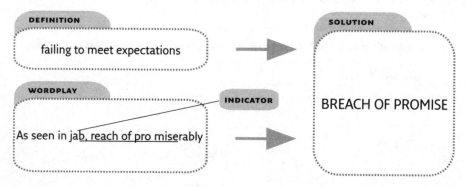

TIP FOR THE TIMES

There may be no **hidden** clue in any one daily puzzle and rarely more than one. This is to avoid the puzzle being too easy but there could well be proportionately more hidden clues in *The Times* jumbo cryptic crossword. Indeed, there does tend to be more flexibility adopted for the jumbos in regard to clueing and other principles.

Finally, for clues requiring the selection of alternate letters, it may be that not all the hidden letters form the whole solution. This is a combination of a **hidden** with an **additive** clue to demonstrate that point:

HIDDEN AND ADDITIVE CLUE: From which spectators watch odd parts of their contest (7)

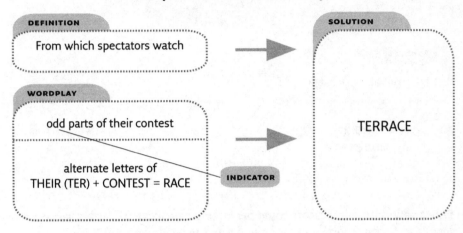

DEFINITION
From which spectators watch

WORDPLAY
odd parts of their contest

alternate letters of
THEIR (TER) + CONTEST = RACE

INDICATOR

SOLUTION
TERRACE

5. The reversal clue: finer points
As indicated earlier, clues can be made up of reversals of more than one word. This one, with its nicely misleading definition, has two reversals:

REVERSAL CLUE (DOWN CLUE): Exotic drama we are mounting – Butler did it (7)

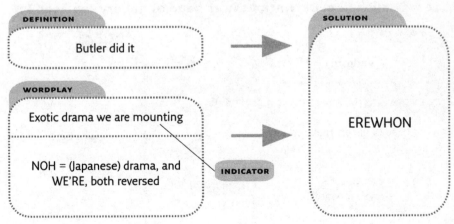

DEFINITION
Butler did it

WORDPLAY
Exotic drama we are mounting

NOH = (Japanese) drama, and
WE'RE, both reversed

INDICATOR

SOLUTION
EREWHON

Also in this category of clue, we include palindromes. Here's an elegant example:

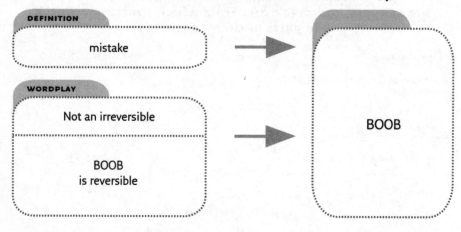

REVERSAL CLUE: Not an irreversible mistake (4)

DEFINITION
mistake

WORDPLAY
Not an irreversible

BOOB
is reversible

BOOB

Other palindrome indicators could be: *looking both ways*, *whichever way you look at it*, *back and forth* (across clue), *up and down* (down clue).

6. The letter switch clue: finer points

The first example is similar to that in Chapter 3 where the letter to be switched is within the clue itself, whereas the second example is harder as the word to be manipulated must be found before the switch can be made:

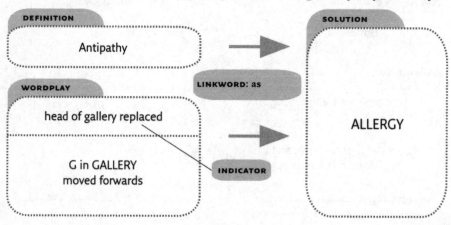

LETTER SWITCH CLUE: Antipathy as head of gallery replaced (7)

DEFINITION
Antipathy

SOLUTION

WORDPLAY
head of gallery replaced

G in GALLERY
moved forwards

LINKWORD: as

INDICATOR

ALLERGY

This second clue is also tougher because the switch indication is the multi-purpose word *for*:

LETTER SWITCH CLUE: Put up with limit after I left for university (9)

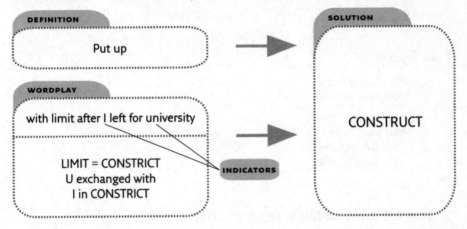

DEFINITION

Put up

WORDPLAY

with limit after I left for university

LIMIT = CONSTRICT
U exchanged with
I in CONSTRICT

INDICATORS

SOLUTION

CONSTRUCT

This use of abbreviations (for example, *good for nothing* would mean *G* replacing *O* in one word to make another), is not uncommon as in the third example below.

LETTER SWITCH CLUE: Like the web? Ladies have a change of heart (5)

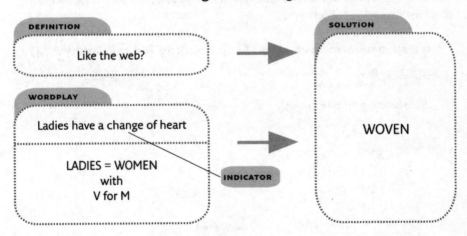

DEFINITION

Like the web?

WORDPLAY

Ladies have a change of heart

LADIES = WOMEN
with
V for M

INDICATOR

SOLUTION

WOVEN

Finally for the next sort of clue, a change of direction may be required as in this nice clue which requires you to switch your thoughts from military matters to boiled eggs:

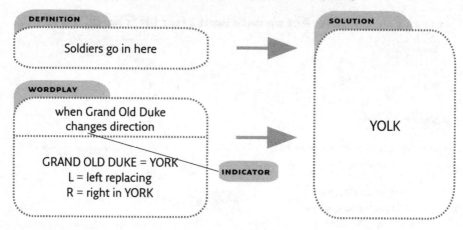

LETTER SWITCH CLUE: Soldiers go in here when grand old duke changes direction (4)

DEFINITION

Soldiers go in here

WORDPLAY

when Grand Old Duke changes direction

GRAND OLD DUKE = YORK
L = left replacing
R = right in YORK

INDICATOR

SOLUTION

YOLK

7. The all-in-one clue: finer points

This clue type has as many subsets as there are types of clue. In other words, the wordplay (remember: always the same as the definition, hence the term **all-in-one**) can take the form of an **anagram**, **additive** or any other sort. Indeed it can even be a combination of these. Here are some examples:

All-in-one additive clue:

The example below shows the clue type at its most concise and the solution requires careful consideration:

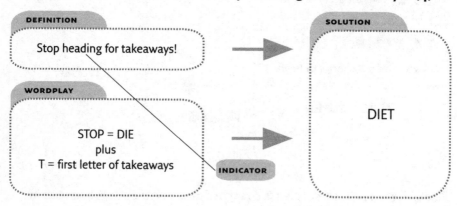

ALL-IN-ONE ADDITIVE CLUE: Stop heading for takeaways! (4)

DEFINITION

Stop heading for takeaways!

WORDPLAY

STOP = DIE
plus
T = first letter of takeaways

INDICATOR

SOLUTION

DIET

All-in-one anagram:
Some nice serendipity is next:

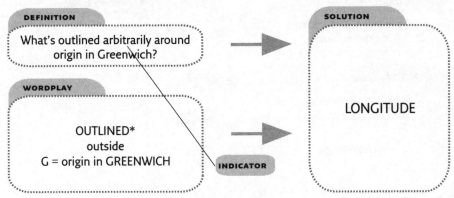

ALL-IN-ONE ANAGRAM AND SANDWICH CLUE:
What's outlined arbitrarily around origin in Greenwich? (9)

DEFINITION

What's outlined arbitrarily around origin in Greenwich?

WORDPLAY

OUTLINED*
outside
G = origin in GREENWICH

INDICATOR

SOLUTION

LONGITUDE

All-in-one anagram and take away:
This involves an **anagram** and **take away** but is still eminently solvable:

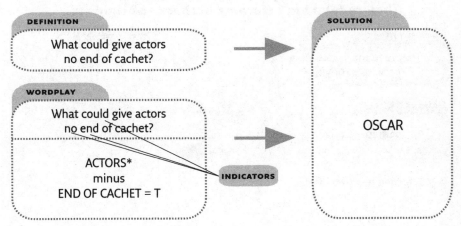

ALL-IN-ONE TAKE AWAY CLUE:
What could give actors no end of cachet? (5)

DEFINITION

What could give actors no end of cachet?

WORDPLAY

What could give actors no end of cachet?

ACTORS*
minus
END OF CACHET = T

INDICATORS

SOLUTION

OSCAR

All-in-one hidden:
The wordplay can be concealed neatly, as here:

ALL-IN-ONE HIDDEN CLUE: What's carried by pupils at Cheltenham? (7)

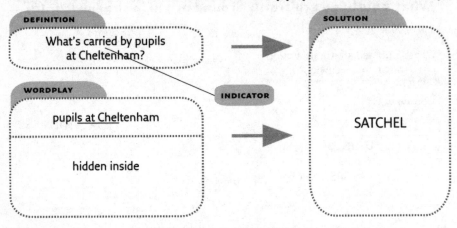

All-in-one hidden and reversal:
The wordplay can also be hidden and reversed with a plural definition:

ALL-IN-ONE HIDDEN AND REVERSAL CLUE:
They're found in returning perhaps to origins (5)

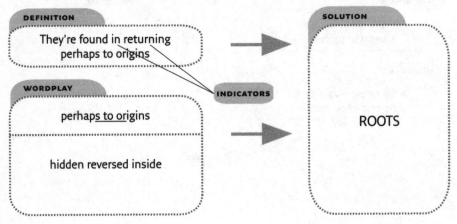

All-in-one sandwich and anagram:

Here the question mark is needed as the solution is only one example of what a shaking duster might collect:

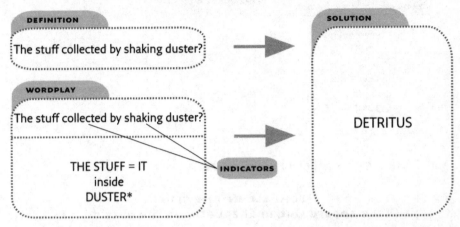

ALL-IN-ONE SANDWICH AND ANAGRAM CLUE:
The stuff collected by shaking duster? (8)

DEFINITION
The stuff collected by shaking duster?

WORDPLAY
The stuff collected by shaking duster?

THE STUFF = IT
inside
DUSTER*

INDICATORS

SOLUTION
DETRITUS

IS THE ALL-IN-ONE CLUE THE MOST SATISFYING?

Setters tend to regard this sort of clue as the pinnacle of clue-writing and it's true that all these examples boast something special with their coincidence of definition and wordplay. However, the **all-in-one** is not necessarily considered so highly by the solvers I meet; their preference is often a clue with a highly misleading image and a pleasingly delayed penny-dropping. In addition, the **all-in-one** may reveal its charms too quickly, especially in the case of the subset discussed next.

There is a variation on the **all-in-one** clue in which the definition is extended by wordplay into a whole sentence. We could think of it as **semi all-in-one**. Solving this type of clue is in principle easier because of the extended definition. Here's one example:

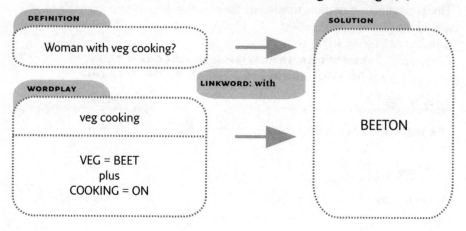

And this neat clue is rather a giveaway, I think:

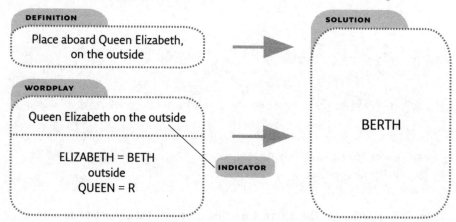

8. The additive clue: finer points

Following a convention established over many years, a *Times* Crossword clue distinguishes between its across or down position in some **additive** clues.

This concerns the word *on* which, as a linkword, means *after* in an across clue and *before* in a down clue, as set out next.

For across clues:

The part that comes first in the solution is placed second in the wordplay. For example, here the *great bloke (top cock)* comes after the *s (for pole)*:

ADDITIVE CLUE (ACROSS): Great bloke on pole, the main controller (8)

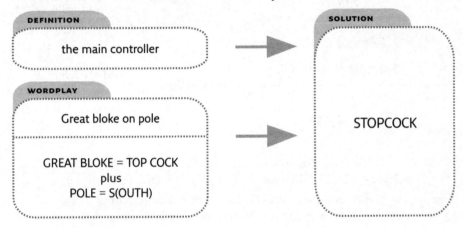

For down clues:

In down clues the parts keep the order of the clue sentence, as with the *was* preceding the *sail = canvas* in this:

ADDITIVE CLUE (DOWN): Festive occasion was put on canvas (7)

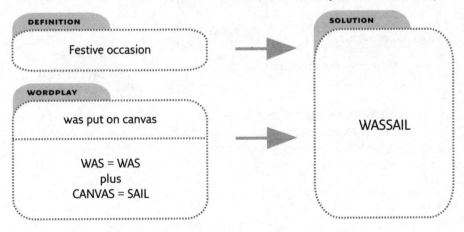

Sometimes the solution word can be broken down into separate parts to form the wordplay. Solving these clues is a question probably of working from the definition back to the wordplay:

ADDITIVE CLUE: Cold display unit for seafood (11)

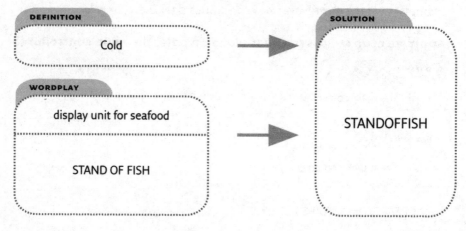

Finally, it will bear repetition from Chapter 3 that the order of the letters or words to be combined may have to be switched, as in the next clue:

ADDITIVE CLUE: Vegetable presented with dessert?
That's a bloomer (5,3)

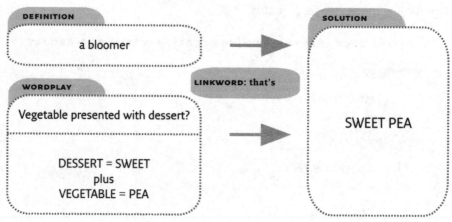

9. The cryptic definition clue: finer points

The more instinctive solver finds this clue one of the easiest; others like me find it the hardest and my practice, once I have recognized the type, is to leave it till later when some solution letters are available. This is especially so when the information given is minimal, as here:

CRYPTIC DEFINITION CLUE: Decline in need of a fall (3,5)

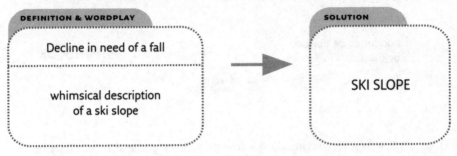

DEFINITION & WORDPLAY

Decline in need of a fall

whimsical description of a ski slope

SOLUTION

SKI SLOPE

This type of wordplay can extend to two misleading words in the clue, as in this example:

CRYPTIC DEFINITION CLUE: What's made only to snap in bits? (7,6)

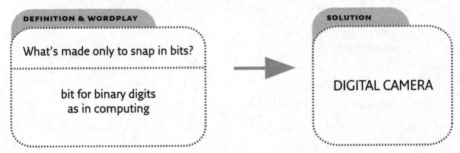

DEFINITION & WORDPLAY

What's made only to snap in bits?

bit for binary digits as in computing

SOLUTION

DIGITAL CAMERA

Occasionally the clue-writer manages to be exceptionally cryptic as here where no fewer than three words have misleading surface meanings:

CRYPTIC DEFINITION CLUE: It's bound to be upheld by those in service (4-4)

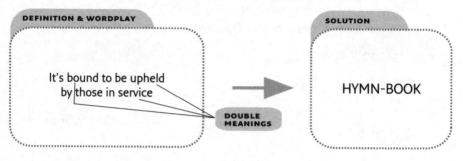

Finally, it is essential to consider each word closely as the solution may be unlocked by putting emphasis on a seemingly unimportant part of the clue, as here:

CRYPTIC DEFINITION CLUE: Help with mental problems one can never get (5,7)

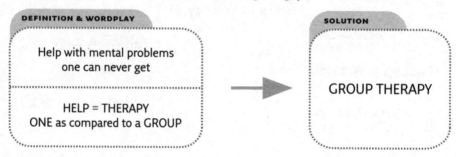

10. The double definition clue: finer points

While these can be recognized from their brevity when there are only two words side by side, they can be longer and harder to spot:

DOUBLE DEFINITION CLUE: A lot of criminals go north of the border (4)

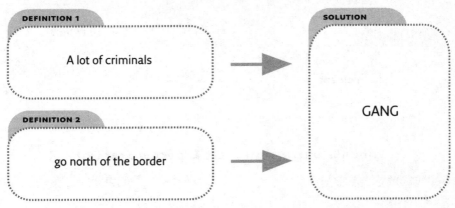

DEFINITION 1

A lot of criminals

DEFINITION 2

go north of the border

SOLUTION

GANG

Also note that there may be one of several possible linkwords between the two or more definitions. *For*, *in* and *is* are three linkword examples in these clues:

DOUBLE DEFINITION CLUE: Responsibility for tax (4)

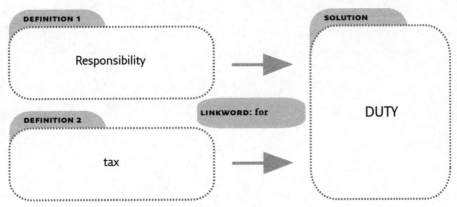

DEFINITION 1

Responsibility

DEFINITION 2

tax

LINKWORD: for

SOLUTION

DUTY

DOUBLE DEFINITION CLUE: Back in a moment (6)

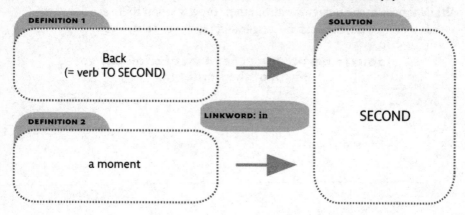

DEFINITION 1

Back
(= verb TO SECOND)

LINKWORD: in

DEFINITION 2

a moment

SOLUTION

SECOND

DOUBLE DEFINITION CLUE: Expert is over (12)

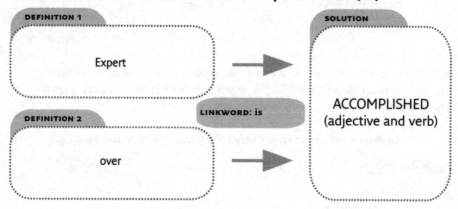

DEFINITION 1

Expert

LINKWORD: is

DEFINITION 2

over

SOLUTION

ACCOMPLISHED
(adjective and verb)

Double definition clues may have a cryptic element in one or other of their parts. Witness this clue:

DOUBLE DEFINITION CLUE: Comfortable job for a boring person (4-2-2)

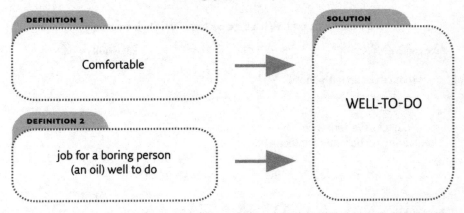

DEFINITION 1

Comfortable

SOLUTION

WELL-TO-DO

DEFINITION 2

job for a boring person
(an oil) well to do

Finally, an example of three definitions which exploit a word with multiple meanings. There is no special tip for finding your way through this ingenious and mischievous wording other than to note that it contains no word that looks anything like an indicator of another clue type:

TRIPLE DEFINITION CLUE: Run some ginger group of similar people (4)

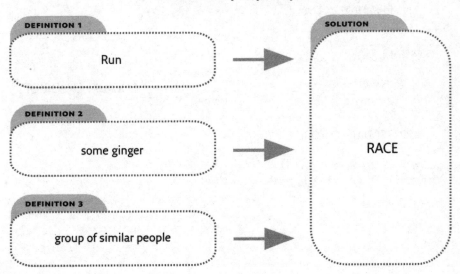

DEFINITION 1

Run

SOLUTION

RACE

DEFINITION 2

some ginger

DEFINITION 3

group of similar people

11. The novelty clue: finer points

By their very nature, these clues defy generalized advice on solving them. There may or may not be an indicator, and there may be an exclamation mark to signal something extraordinary. Otherwise it's a question of thinking 'out of the box':

NOVELTY CLUE: What cooks do with books (5)

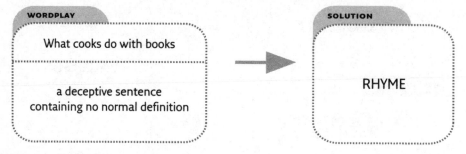

The next example is a rare but agreeable case of something concealed as an abbreviation (NaCl) within part of the wordplay which, unabbreviated, gives the solution:

NOVELTY CLUE: It's found in the ocean and briefly in barnacles (6,8)

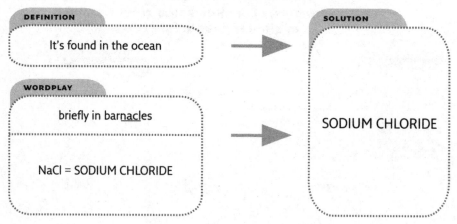

In the next example, the clue-writer exploits the repetition of letters (*S,E,A,T*) within the solution, and incidentally finds a one-word definition (*calm*) in a different part of speech to that of the solution. The message is: ignore the definitional part of speech.

NOVELTY CLUE: Calm constituents in a seat, two or three times (3,2,4)

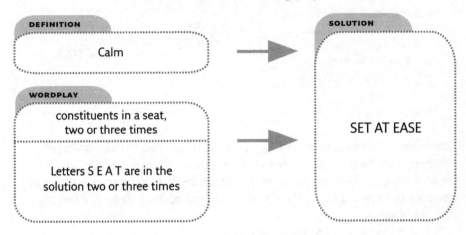

Next, you must split the solution into two parts and imagine it as a slogan supporting the Queen.

NOVELTY CLUE: Servant's anti-republican slogan? (8)

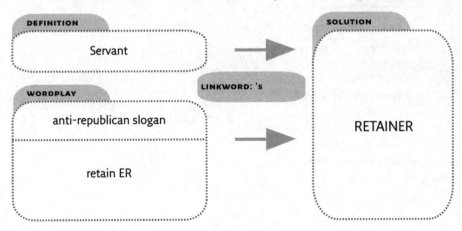

Here is a really 'off-the-wall' clue which, strictly speaking, is defective in that it lacks a definition. However, it's fun and would presumably have led to warm glows of satisfaction when the penny dropped:

NOVELTY CLUE: My first is what my second is not (7)

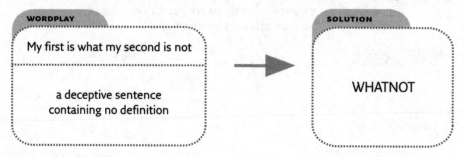

WORDPLAY

My first is what my second is not

a deceptive sentence containing no definition

SOLUTION

WHATNOT

Under this heading we can include clues which use the verbal twisting of William Archibald Spooner. He was an Anglican clergyman and Warden of New College, Oxford, whose nervous manner led him to utter many slips of the tongue, especially involving comic reversals such as Queer old Dean for Dear old Queen.

This is an example of a clue in this style :

NOVELTY CLUE: Lowest possible cost of jam and cereal for Spooner (7,5)

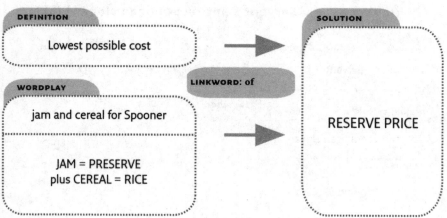

DEFINITION

Lowest possible cost

LINKWORD: of

WORDPLAY

jam and cereal for Spooner

JAM = PRESERVE
plus CEREAL = RICE

SOLUTION

RESERVE PRICE

Here is a favoured clue that is perhaps more of a riddle than a clue:

NOVELTY CLUE: If one cold toe is numb, two must be _____ (4,6)

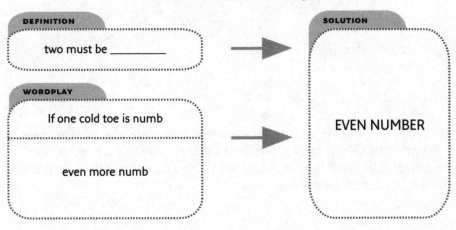

Last, I have lost count of the number of times people have given me their favourite clue. It is a symbolic representation rather than a clue and evidently appeared many years ago.

NOVELTY CLUE: H I J K L M N O (5)

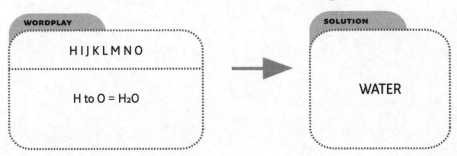

Its extension, listed next, appeared more recently and might tickle your fancy:

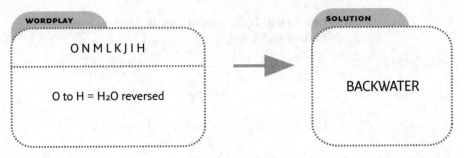

NOVELTY CLUE: O N M L K J I H (9)

WORDPLAY

ONMLKJIH

O to H = H₂O reversed

SOLUTION

BACKWATER

As you will have observed from the examples above, **novelty** clues are mostly 'one-offs' and solving them is therefore a matter of inspiration rather than technique. They tend to be especially enjoyable and, as you gain experience, you will spot them more easily.

9. Finer Points of Clues: General

'Often a single word betrays a great design.' Racine

Now to some points that are unrelated to specific clue types.

1. More complex constructions

Until now we have been concerned mainly with demonstrating how to solve clues that have one element of trickery within them. Many clues do follow this pattern but should you be daunted by those which do not? I'd say not at all: it's just a question of needing to decode the separate elements, each of which will be signalled in its own way. Even if the word defined is an unusual one and the wordplay complex, you can follow the indicators eventually to arrive at the solution. The complex clue is reserved usually for intractable words (as in the following clue), for which the setter can find no alternative. Don't worry if you find this too difficult as simplicity is the norm in *The Times* Crossword – a horrendous clue like this is not that common:

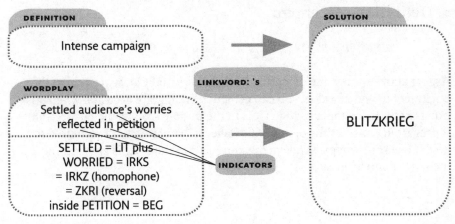

COMPLEX CLUE – SANDWICH INCLUDING REVERSAL AND HOMOPHONE: Intense campaign's settled audience's worries reflected in petition (10)

DEFINITION

Intense campaign

LINKWORD: 's

SOLUTION

BLITZKRIEG

WORDPLAY

Settled audience's worries reflected in petition

SETTLED = LIT plus
WORRIED = IRKS
= IRKZ (homophone)
= ZKRI (reversal)
inside PETITION = BEG

INDICATORS

This next clue was also tough to solve when I first saw it, not least because it is constructed with the unusual word *lower* (see Chapter 10). Also, it has no linking words (it's always harder without them), and *Sgt Lewis*, looking as if the two words must go together in a definition, does in fact need separating into two parts.

COMPLEX CLUE – SANDWICH: Lower rent houses for Sgt Lewis maybe here? (11)

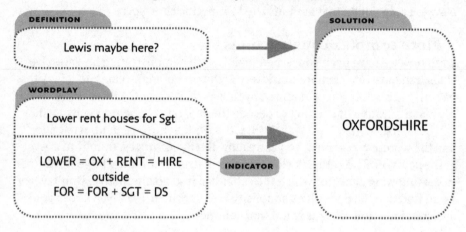

DEFINITION

Lewis maybe here?

WORDPLAY

Lower rent houses for Sgt

LOWER = OX + RENT = HIRE
outside
FOR = FOR + SGT = DS

INDICATOR

SOLUTION

OXFORDSHIRE

Faced with either of the above two clues, I'd certainly recommend deferral until some intersecting help was available.

2. Definition placement

'*I hate definitions.*' Benjamin Disraeli, *Vivian Gray*

As you know by now, the definition in clues is virtually always either at the beginning or end of a clue; you can get stuck on the rare occasion when it is not. Next is an example in which it is in the middle. You would be forgiven for regarding *instil* as the definition. However, you are actually required to read it like this: when a solution meaning part of the body is anagrammed, it changes into *instil awe*.

ANAGRAM CLUE: Instil awe when this part of the body is fantastic! (9)

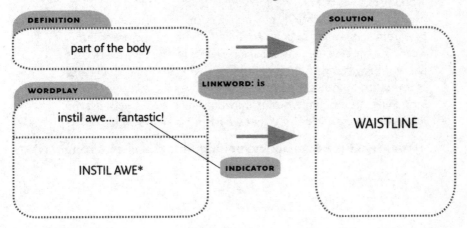

DEFINITION

part of the body

WORDPLAY

instil awe... fantastic!

INSTIL AWE*

LINKWORD: is

INDICATOR

SOLUTION

WAISTLINE

3. Linkwords

Fairly commonly, the linkword has to be taken as one form in the surface reading and a different form in the wordplay. In this example, the use of 's means possessive pronoun in the former and *is* in the latter.

SANDWICH CLUE: Prostitute's 'leave it alone' as bottom's pinched (8)

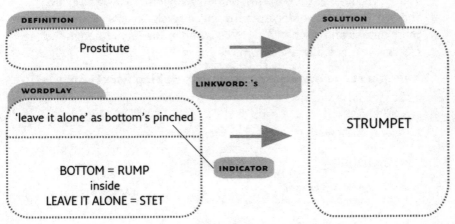

DEFINITION

Prostitute

WORDPLAY

'leave it alone' as bottom's pinched

BOTTOM = RUMP
inside
LEAVE IT ALONE = STET

LINKWORD: 's

INDICATOR

SOLUTION

STRUMPET

TIP FOR THE TIMES

Working out which way the linkword is pointing can be tricky. For example, while it is entirely normal (in normal English and crosswords) that *from* and *leading to* point to the answer from the preceding wordplay, the reverse may occasionally apply. The test is whether the wordplay stands for the definition: that is to say, it clearly and grammatically shows the process which gives the solution. By stretching the language, some linkwords such as *get*, *gets*, *getting*, *makes* or *making* can point either way. Here is an example:

ANAGRAM CLUE: Fiscal policy making Americans go wrong? (11)

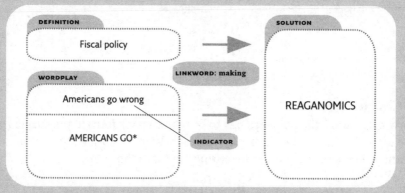

You are required to think of the solution giving rise to the **anagram fodder**. The reverse order, as in my reworked clue below, would be more natural and is more likely to be found in *The Times* (though the clue above is actually taken from *The Times*).

ANAGRAM CLUE: Americans go wrong making fiscal policy (11)

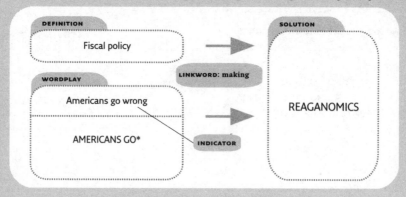

4. Punctuation: misleading

Apart from question marks and exclamation marks (see next paragraph), punctuation is by convention in all crosswords unreliable. This is especially confusing to beginners who have to be reminded that it may mislead and may have to be ignored. For example, the components of an anagram can be split across a full stop or a comma.

MISLEADING PUNCTUATION – ANAGRAM CLUE:
Exciting parcel, and she barely moves close (3,6)

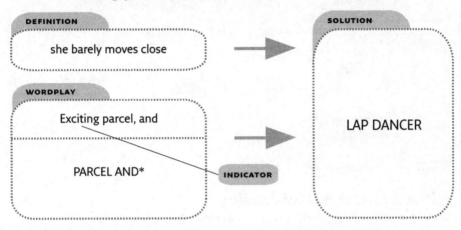

DEFINITION: she barely moves close

WORDPLAY: Exciting parcel, and
PARCEL AND*
INDICATOR

SOLUTION: LAP DANCER

Or punctuation can mislead by separating the parts to be initialized, i.e. first letters are to be taken from words either side of the comma, as seen here:

MISLEADING PUNCTUATION – ADDITIVE CLUE:
Diamonds are real, asked initially – sauce! (9)

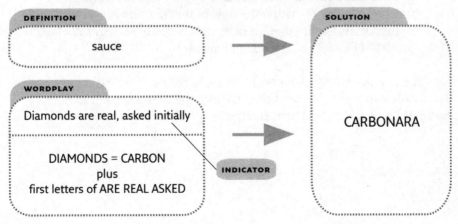

DEFINITION: sauce

WORDPLAY: Diamonds are real, asked initially
DIAMONDS = CARBON
plus
first letters of ARE REAL ASKED
INDICATOR

SOLUTION: CARBONARA

Punctuation can be omitted, too, as here where the comma required by the cryptic reading between the last two words (as in 'I, say') is not shown in the second definition:

MISLEADING PUNCTUATION – DOUBLE DEFINITION CLUE:
'Excellent', I say (7)

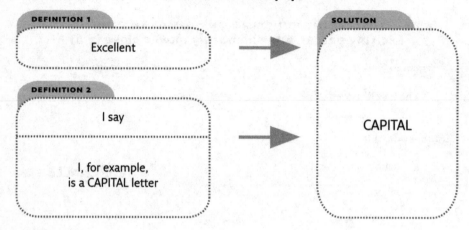

DEFINITION 1

Excellent

DEFINITION 2

I say

I, for example,
is a CAPITAL letter

SOLUTION

CAPITAL

5. Punctuation: not misleading

The exceptions when punctuation is there to help are mainly in these two cases:

- **Question mark**: as a hint that the solution either is slightly tenuous, or it's an example of a group rather than a synonym. Thus *apple* to define *fruit* may well have a question mark.
- **Exclamation mark**: as an indication either that something most unusual is going on within the clue, or that the clue has a remarkable or humorous feature that the setter wants you especially to notice, albeit not in a self-congratulatory manner.

Occasionally, punctuation is included to make the deciphering of the wordplay clearer, as in the next clue in which the commas point to the two parts to be added (and incidentally the *of* = *o'* or *o*).

HELPFUL PUNCTUATION – ADDITIVE CLUE INCLUDING SANDWICH:
It's put on bow of ship, initially, one in the navy (5)

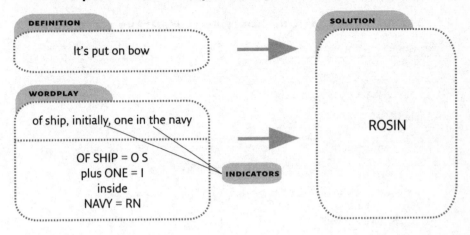

DEFINITION

It's put on bow

SOLUTION

WORDPLAY

of ship, initially, one in the navy

OF SHIP = O S
plus ONE = I
inside
NAVY = RN

INDICATORS

ROSIN

WHAT DO ELLIPSES IN CLUES MEAN?

I'm often asked this at workshops. It's so simple that I suspect people are looking for something more tricky than it is. It's merely a way of connecting two clues (sometimes more) to present a longer than normal clue sentence, i.e. across the two clues. Each clue stands on its own with regard to definition and wordplay. Here is an example:

TWO CLUES LINKED BY ELLIPSES:
5 down: Annoyed on account of one bird... (9)
6 down: ...fleeces others (5)

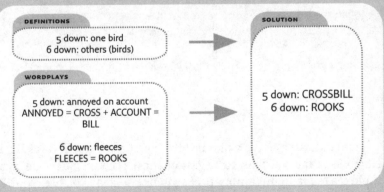

DEFINITIONS
5 down: one bird
6 down: others (birds)

WORDPLAYS

5 down: annoyed on account
ANNOYED = CROSS + ACCOUNT =
BILL

6 down: fleeces
FLEECES = ROOKS

SOLUTION

5 down: CROSSBILL
6 down: ROOKS

Finally, here is an example of punctuation not only being helpful but forming the definition:

HELPFUL PUNCTUATION - ADDITIVE CLUE: Argue score? (8,4)

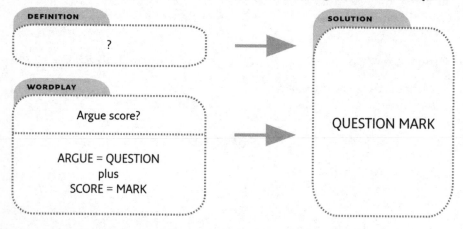

6. Crossword grammar

Anagrams can be indicated by either a singular or a plural verb. Consider this example:

ANAGRAM CLUE: Can the old play in this competition? (9)

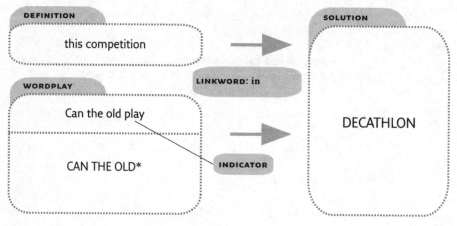

The anagram indicator *play* is a plural verb whereas you might think it needs to be singular for the wordplay to be grammatical. It could indeed be so but that would make for an ungrammatical sentence; instead you are required to consider the **anagram fodder** to be individual letters which then play (or change) before the solution is unravelled.

Another typical example of crossword grammar is in defining adjectives with an 's. In the clue below, the apostrophe looks at first glance as though it may be a **linkword** (for *is*) but in fact it's an adjectival synonym for the solution.

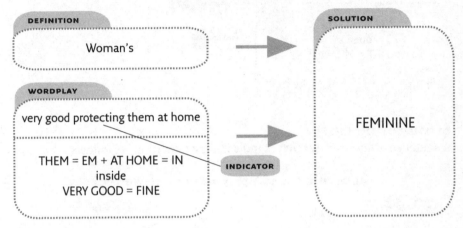

SANDWICH CLUE: Woman's very good protecting them at home (8)

DEFINITION

Woman's

WORDPLAY

very good protecting them at home

THEM = EM + AT HOME = IN
inside
VERY GOOD = FINE

INDICATOR

SOLUTION

FEMININE

7. Crossword war horses

There are inevitably some crossword terms that occur time and again, often words of two, three or four letter words. It is impossible to list all of them here but those in this P. G. Wodehouse quotation (from *Meet Mr Mulliner*) may still be seen today:

> '*George spent his evenings doing the crossword puzzle. By the time he was thirty he knew more about Eli, the prophet, Ra the Sun God and the bird Emu than anybody else in the country except the vicar's daughter who had also taken up the solving of crossword puzzles and was the first girl in Worcestershire to find out the meaning of stearine and crepuscular.*'

An appropriately named military war horse is the US General who is still honoured, as in this next clue:

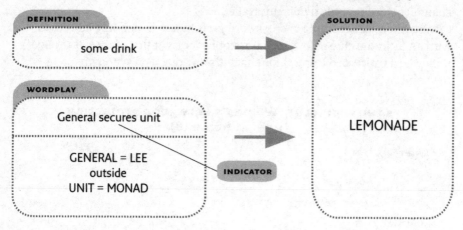

SANDWICH CLUE: General secures unit some drink (8)

DEFINITION

some drink

SOLUTION

WORDPLAY

General secures unit

GENERAL = LEE
outside
UNIT = MONAD

INDICATOR

LEMONADE

8. Stuttering clues

A sentence uttered stutteringly is indicated by repetition, as follows:

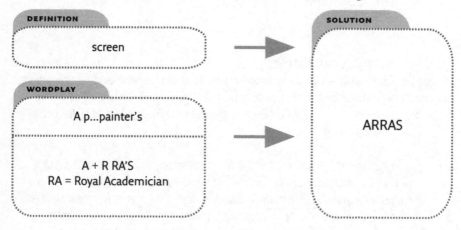

ADDITIVE CLUE: A p...painter's screen (5)

DEFINITION

screen

SOLUTION

WORDPLAY

A p...painter's

A + R RA'S
RA = Royal Academician

ARRAS

9. Use of first person singular

An inanimate object can be defined as if it were a person. This rather nice clue is an example:

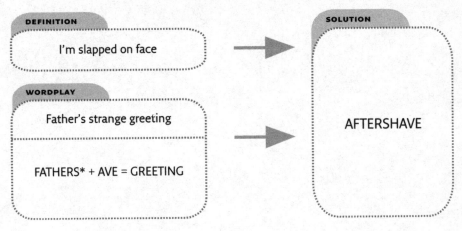

ADDITIVE CLUE: Father's strange greeting –
I'm slapped on face (10)

DEFINITION

I'm slapped on face

WORDPLAY

Father's strange greeting

FATHERS* + AVE = GREETING

SOLUTION

AFTERSHAVE

10. Ten Especially Troublesome Words

'The idlest way of passing an hour I can think of is doing the crossword. It occupies the mind without overtaxing the brain. It has a slightly virtuous air to it, the feeling that you are doing something rather more useful than playing patience.' Keith Waterhouse, *Saga* magazine

Either because they have multiple uses, or because they are a well-established convention but not immediately obvious, there are a few particularly awkward words which it's good to know about. The first two, *about* and *in*, are especially difficult for newcomers.

1. About
One of the most misleading words in crosswords is *about* because it has so many uses:
- a **reversal** indicator of whole words, or parts of them, in across and down clues
- a **sandwich** indicator
- an **anagram** indicator
- *C, CA* as abbreviations
- a synonym for *re* and *on*

2. In
Likewise the innocent little multi-purpose word *in* causes trouble. Each of these next seven clues uses *in* differently. First, as a **hidden** indicator:

HIDDEN CLUE: In Amritsar, it's a common habit (4)

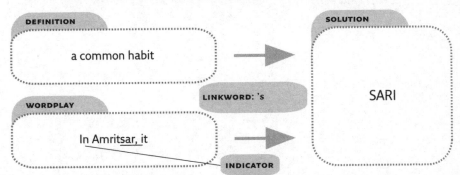

DEFINITION

a common habit

WORDPLAY

In Amritsar, it

LINKWORD: 's

INDICATOR

SOLUTION

SARI

Second, as a **linkword** between definition and wordplay:

ADDITIVE CLUE: **Be prolific in area before spring (6)**

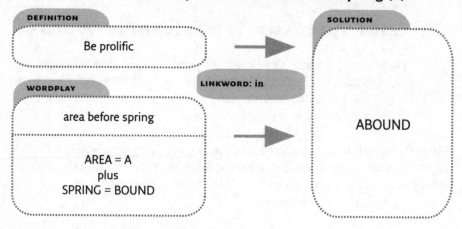

Third, as a **sandwich** indicator:

SANDWICH CLUE: **Clearly aren't in use (10)**

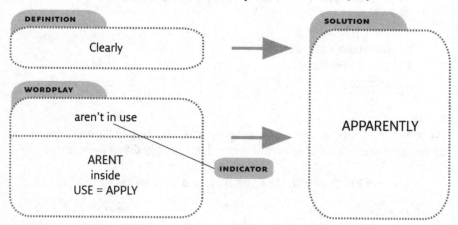

Fourth, as a **definition**:

SANDWICH CLUE: In goal, blocking attempt (6)

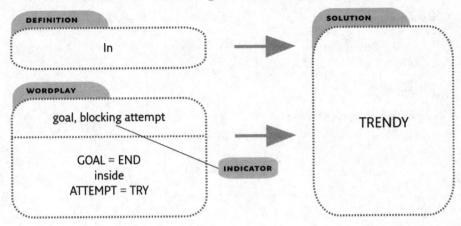

DEFINITION

In

WORDPLAY

goal, blocking attempt

GOAL = END
inside
ATTEMPT = TRY

INDICATOR

SOLUTION

TRENDY

Fifth, as a **definition** in another language:

CRYPTIC DEFINITION: This is in French (2,7)

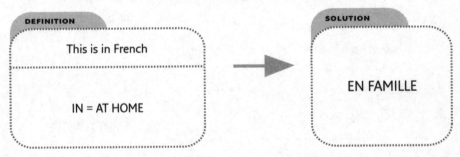

DEFINITION

This is in French

IN = AT HOME

SOLUTION

EN FAMILLE

Sixth, as part of the **definition**:

HOMOPHONE CLUE: One in bed reciting numbers of sheep (5)

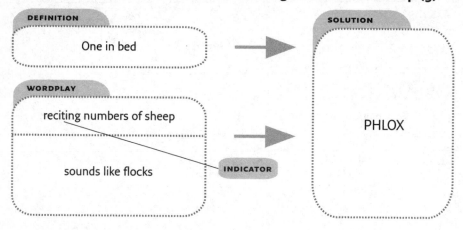

DEFINITION
One in bed

WORDPLAY
reciting numbers of sheep

sounds like flocks

INDICATOR

SOLUTION
PHLOX

Seventh, as part of the **wordplay**:

ADDITIVE CLUE: Cover up furniture in court case (9)

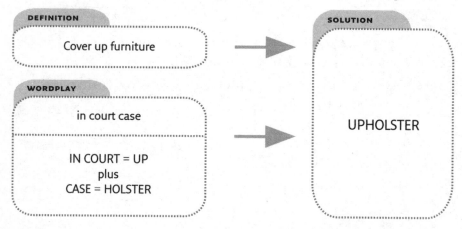

DEFINITION
Cover up furniture

WORDPLAY
in court case

IN COURT = UP
plus
CASE = HOLSTER

SOLUTION
UPHOLSTER

3. Without

This can be an indication that something must be taken away, as below:

TAKE AWAY CLUE: Drink that's sweet, without ice (6)

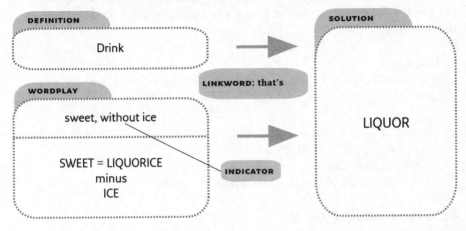

In *The Times* Crossword, as in many other puzzles, *without* is also used in the sense of *outside* (marked as archaic in most dictionaries). It is therefore a **sandwich** indicator, as follows:

SANDWICH CLUE: Gardens without nitrogen can be recognized (4)

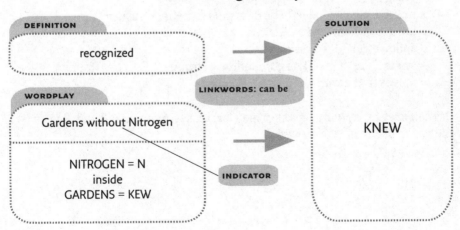

4. One

The word *one* can be a substitute for *I*, *ace* and *un* (from the dialect usage *'un*) but not normally *a* nor *an*. Though this is supported by dictionaries, *The Times* follows its long-standing convention. A rare exception is where *one* forms part of a phrase, for example, *one fine day*, which might include *one* to be taken as *A* in wordplay.

5. Men

In *The Times* Crossword, men are more trouble than women. Here are some usages:

- *man* can be *he*, a chess piece or pawn, a soldier, an island as in the Isle of Man, or just a plain fellow
- *male* can be *m* or *he*
- *men* may need converting to *or* (for *other ranks*)

6. Words ending in -er

In the sometimes artificial world of crosswords, we can encounter nouns with unexpected, arguably unnatural, meanings that are implied rather than overtly specified in dictionaries.

Here are some which can serve to indicate anything that:

- flows, e.g. a river or stream – *flower*
- blooms, e.g. a flower – *bloomer*
- numbs, e.g. an anaesthetic or an anaesthetist – *number*
- lows, e.g. a cow, an ox – *lower*
- splits, e.g. a tool – *river*
- strains, e.g. tug-of-war competitor – *strainer*
- moves in the water, e.g. fish – *swimmer*

In *The Times* Crossword, a banker may live in, say, Switzerland and also on the banks of a river, as follows:

ADDITIVE (DOWN) CLUE INCLUDING REVERSAL:
Love to upset an African banker (5)

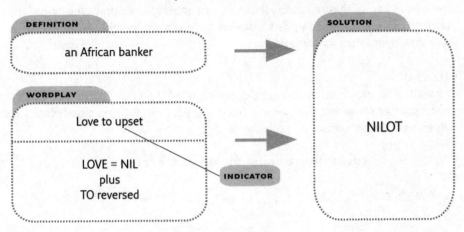

DEFINITION

an African banker

WORDPLAY

Love to upset

LOVE = NIL
plus
TO reversed

INDICATOR

SOLUTION

NILOT

7. Of

Of can very occasionally be a linking word between the solution and wordplay.
Its meaning in this case is stretched to *from* or *constituted by* as here in this –
probably rare – *Times* Crossword example:

SANDWICH (DOWN) CLUE: Look up prehistoric city in an issue of learning (9)

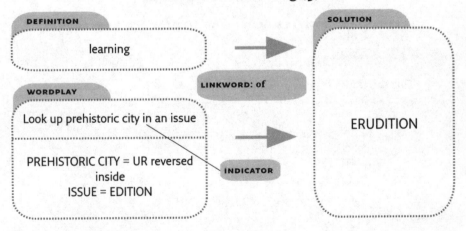

DEFINITION

learning

LINKWORD: of

WORDPLAY

Look up prehistoric city in an issue

PREHISTORIC CITY = UR reversed
inside
ISSUE = EDITION

INDICATOR

SOLUTION

ERUDITION

8. & 9. Right and left

Right and *left* appear in a number of guises. *Right* can be an anagram indicator (= verb, *to correct*); the letter *r* as an abbreviation; and synonyms such as *ok* and *lien*. *Left* can be a **take away** indicator; the abbreviation *l*; and synonyms such as *over* and *port*.

10. Say

As well as its most common usage as a synonym for *for example* or *e.g.*, the word *say* can show that the clue is a homophone, as in the first clue below, or it can be a simple synonym, as in the second:

HOMOPHONE CLUE: Shrub or trees, say (5)

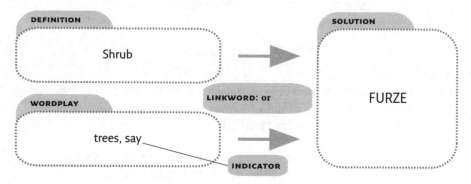

ALL-IN-ONE ADDITIVE CLUE: One to produce key, say (6)

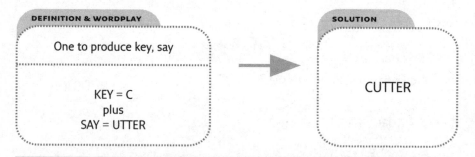

KEY NOTES

The word *key* (as in the previous clue) and its sister, *note*, can have a lot of forms (some argue unfairly) in their various musical guises. As regards phonetic notes, they are these: *do, doh, re, mi, me, fa, so, soh, la, lah, te, ti*; or they can be single letters: *a, b, c, d, e, f, g*.

11: Tips for *The Times*

'Fellas were like easy crosswords; you knew the answers before you'd finished the questions, and they usually weren't worth doing.' Roddy Doyle,
The Woman Who Walked Into Doors

All crosswords have features that are specific to their newspaper or are shared by only a few. Some of these have been shown in boxes alongside a relevant explanation; in addition there are some more general points for *The Times* Crossword.

The philosophy at *The Times* has always been that 'rules' are not set in stone. This is largely so as not to inhibit the ingenuity and creativity of setters. What follows therefore is to be taken against that background and is supplementary to the general principles set out earlier. Some of these points may be helpful to anyone transferring their crossword affections from another newspaper:

- The names of living people are not generally found, with the exception of the Queen who can be *R*, *ER* or *HM*.

- Though you will not expect to see living people, commercial names, trademarks and other forms of advertising in *The Times* Crossword, the following may appear: national newspapers and periodicals, political parties and not-for-profit organizations such as the National Trust, the UN and the Salvation Army.

- If, by exception, an American usage or spelling is part of a clue, it will usually be indicated as such, as in the clue overleaf:

CRYPTIC DEFINITION CLUE: One may move on to another American story (9)

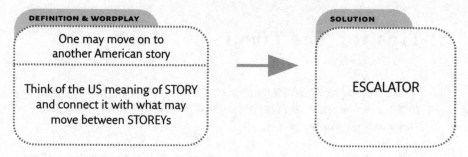

DEFINITION & WORDPLAY

One may move on to another American story

Think of the US meaning of STORY and connect it with what may move between STOREYs

SOLUTION

ESCALATOR

- A nounal phrase is used as a letter selection indicator. For example, *Times Leader* can indicate the letter *T* (which, incidentally, is required to be expressed as *Times's Leader* or *Leader in Times* according to principles interpreted from Ximenes in, say, the *Observer* series of Azed and Everyman).

- In a similar vein, nouns alongside the **anagram fodder** may indicate an **anagram**, as here:

ANAGRAM CLUE: Vocalist needs rare arrangement (9)

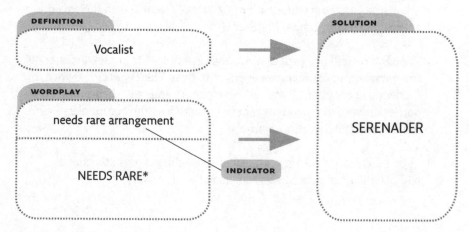

DEFINITION

Vocalist

SOLUTION

SERENADER

WORDPLAY

needs rare arrangement

NEEDS RARE*

INDICATOR

- There is more precision with regard to some aspects of letter selection indicators in *The Times* Crossword than elsewhere. For example, *a bit of cheek* is not used to indicate a first letter *c*; *start working* is not used to indicate *w*, for which *start of work* is the more grammatical norm.

- A typical *Times* puzzle is not littered with literary references as is commonly assumed, but rather has a balanced mixture of clue subjects. Analysis by bloggers (see Chapter 15 for the *timesforthetimes* blog) shows that there are likely to be as many references to, say, popular culture as there are to literature.

- **Apostrophes** are considered as part of the word they relate to. Thus, *raison d'être* is shown as two words, not three, and its word-length would be (6,5). This can make a solution much harder to find.

- As mentioned earlier, *one* in a clue's wordplay in *The Times* Crossword can indicate *i* but not *a*.

- International Vehicle Registrations (for example, CH for Switzerland) do not feature as abbreviations, at least as part of the wordplay, although they may exceptionally feature as part of a definition (as seen in one of the 'Clues to Try' on page 149).

- Though the puzzle is widely syndicated, its perspective is firmly British as shown in this example:

TAKE AWAY CLUE: Disheartened fighter once our enemy (4)

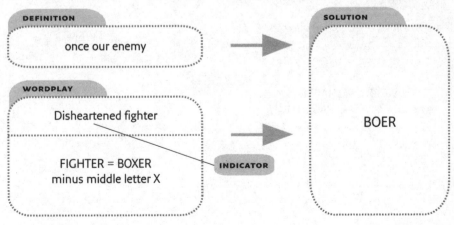

DEFINITION

once our enemy

SOLUTION

WORDPLAY

Disheartened fighter

FIGHTER = BOXER
minus middle letter X

INDICATOR

BOER

- Numerals in *Times* clues always refer to another clue in the puzzle and not to a number in another form, e.g. *10* does not become *X* as is the case in, say, the *Guardian*.

- If you are an internet solver, beware occasional, annoying differences between *The Times* Crossword Club online and the newspaper in regard to numbers. For example, *M25* in one of the practice puzzles appears as *M Twenty Five* in the former version.

- Occasionally the language of an indicator is stretched totally from the normal meaning of a word. In the clue below, the word *outraged* (which one might initially regard as an **anagram** indicator) is in fact an indication that *raged* must be removed from *tragedy* to leave the letters *ty*. Thus the solver must split the word into two parts and reverse them, before an instruction (*raged out*) can be elicited. If extended to any word (e.g. *indeed* interpreted as a **sandwich** indicator for letters *de-* and *-ed* in a clue to *deformed*), this could make solving even harder, so instances where normal English usage is abandoned are likely to be seen in only a few outrageous clues such as this one.

SANDWICH CLUE INCLUDING TAKE AWAY:
Figure exited amid tragedy when outraged (6)

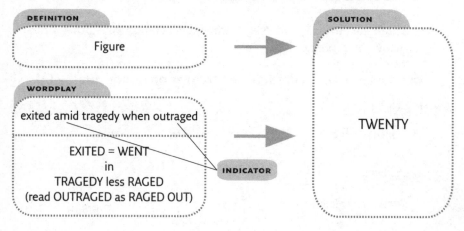

DEFINITION

Figure

SOLUTION

WORDPLAY

exited amid tragedy when outraged

EXITED = WENT
in
TRAGEDY less RAGED
(read OUTRAGED as RAGED OUT)

INDICATOR

TWENTY

12: A Solving Sequence

'*I wish he would explain his explanation.*' Lord Byron, *Don Juan*

In this chapter I take a typical *Times* Crossword and record my solving process. I would not claim that it's the only way of solving, nor that it is especially fast. Having been totally outclassed in the only *Times* solving competition I entered, I don't claim to be a brilliant solver and, as you will see, I got stuck a couple of times. Also you will see that sometimes I flit around the grid rather than follow letters already uncovered. That usually indicates that I can go no further with available letters and am effectively starting afresh.

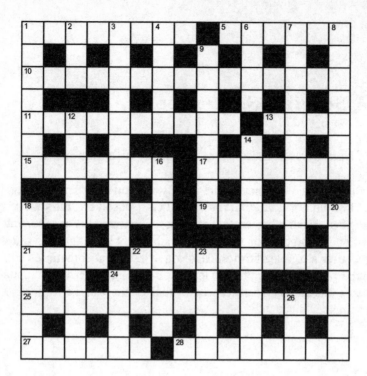

Across

1 After first from college, mocking illicit exam technique (8)
5 Untidily throws down second pair of trousers (6)
10 Hairy thing, war with USA - so much let off (6,9)
11 Pound: an offer given in a hurry to be trusted (3-7)
13 What's turned out from recipes is impressive (4)
15 Comedian appears better touring the South (7)
17 Without passing judgment, peer shows uprightness (7)
18 Men and their English homes? (7)
19 Locker moving a nut into place when turned (7)
21 Noble king pushing crown to the back (4)
22 He's quick to put top hat on President's head (4-6)
25 Deception might become kind of eccentric (10,5)
27 Design paraded? (6)
28 A kitchen device each minute pocketed by thief? (3-5)

Down

1 One bloomer has to threaten another (7)
2 Don't open medicine, though in need of it? (3)
3 Down every glug - get a buzz out of it! (10)
4 Uncertain character, though certainly not unbalanced (5)
6 Popular mummy beginning to undo skirt (4)
7 Is a departure so good? (11)
8 Imprecise score written in blue (7)
9 Old servant becomes mine (8)
12 Is one tied at royal wedding? (7,4)
14 One carried out when another carried off? (10)
16 Male breaking his family up put on further performance (8)
18 Style in which redundancies effected? (4,3)
20 Forward one out? (7)
23 Announcer, male, beginning to check through similar notes (5)
24 As a down-and-out, always be a loser? (4)
26 Like a smooth thing, doffing cap (3)

So where to start? I look for the longest words as, clearly, solving one will give many intersecting letters to work on.

10a Hairy thing, war with USA – so much let off (6,9)

This looks like an **anagram** with *off* as the indicator, and a letter-count of the **fodder** shows 15 letters in *war usa so much let*. The punctuation within these words and the **linkword** *with* are both to be ignored, as so often is the case. So what's the definition? Must be *hairy thing*. Can it be some sort of *moustache*? Yes, leaving *warusl*, so *walrus* it is.

Rarely with two 15-letter words in one crossword are both doable quickly, nor would one expect another **anagram**, but let's look at 25 across which has *might become*, a possible **angram** indicator.

25a Deception might become kind of eccentric (10,5)

There are 15 letters in *kind of eccentric*. As the solution is (10,5) there is a better chance of cracking it than if it were a 15-letter solution; so taking the definition as *deception*, could the second word be *trick*? Spot on, and it leaves *confidence* to complete the answer. A very good clue, don't you think? Short, smooth sentence and yes, deceptive; but not for us!

So, there are lots of letters to work with now:

Three-letter words are often easier than most so let's try 2 and 26 down:

2d Don't open medicine, though in need of it? (3)
26d Like a smooth thing, doffing cap (3)

Don't open looks like a **take away** indicator so is there a four-letter word that, with its first letter deducted, gives a word connected with *need*ing medicine? *Pill* becomes *ill* so that's put in. 26 down starts with *I* and there aren't many words that would fit there. Furthermore, it's another **take away** (*doffing cap*) but does that give the answer? Not yet, and it's not too certain what the definition is, so let's leave it for now.

5a Untidily throws down second pair of trousers (6)

Try 5 across as that may well end in *s* (*throws down* and *trousers*) but no joy. However, the final *s* will give us the first letter of 8 down, so let's put that in.

8d Imprecise score written in blue (6)

Could be an **additive** or a **sandwich** type. If the latter, then a three-letter synonym of *blue* starting with *s* must be *sky*. So how about *sketchy* which would be *imprecise*? That leaves *etch* = *score*. Perhaps a little imprecise itself but clearly we have the solution.

13a What's turned out from recipes is impressive (4)
Four-letter word ending in *c*? There cannot be many of those and the clue type may well be **hidden** plus a **reversal** (remember that two clue types can be combined in one clue). *Epic* is there and that's *impressive* (not all that impressive, you might think, as it's a pretty easy clue as most **hiddens** are).

7d Is a departure so good? (11)
This looks within reach – let's try *A* or *I* as the first letter and see what might be a **double definition** clue. No luck, so look for an unusual letter in a good position. It could be 1 down:

1d One bloomer has to threaten another (7)
Bloomer often signifies a flower. Quite a hard clue but, *slip* also being a *bloomer*, *cowslip* comes to mind. OK but why? We must work backwards from the guess and *cow* = *threaten* goes with *slip* = *bloomer* for the justification.

First letters are nearly always the most valuable, so to 15 next.

15a Comedian appears better touring the South (7)
Touring gives us a **sandwich** probably and we know it has *s* (for *south*) in it. A *comedian* is a punster but why *better*? A deceptive way of clueing *punter* – easy when you see it eventually!

WALRUSMOUSTACHE
EPIC
PUNSTER
CONFIDENCETRICK
COWSLIP
SKETCHY
IL

Surely 1 across is next?

1a After first from college, mocking illicit exam technique (8)
An **additive** *c* plus *ribbing* = *mocking* gives the *illicit exam technique* fairly swiftly.

Seeking valuable first letters, let's try 4 down next. This clue must be easy and so it proves:

4d Uncertain character, though certainly not unbalanced (5)
The setter's friendly *nomad* puts in an appearance after his wandering. *Not unbalanced* gives us the *no mad* split and we're confident of the answer. We could have just written in *nomad* based on *unsettled character* but that can be a bad idea if we guess wrongly. After all, the whole raison d'être is to deceive and it's safer to check both definition and wordplay. You can get awfully held up by solutions inked in that prove to be wrong.

3d Down every glug – get a buzz out of it! (10)
This looked initially like an anagram (with *d* = *down*) but it can't be now. A *buzz* comes from *insects* so must be *bluebottle*. So *down* = *blue*, does it? Yes, as depressed, etc., and *every glug* = (the whole) *bottle*. Nice one, eh?

18d Style in which redundancies effected? (4,3)
Looks eminently solvable with the three-letter part being *cut*; so it's a short step to *crew cut* and that opens up 18 across.

18a Men and their English homes? (7)
English homes obviously means *castles* and the second definition refers to chess(men). Easiest one so far. Some solvers, preferring a quick scan of all the clues, may well alight on this one first.

On the basis that four intersecting letters in a (7,4) word must be most helpful, let's go to 12 down because that will surely enable completion of 11 across.

12d Is one tied at royal wedding? (7,4)
Could be *knot* to end with and thence the *Windsor* connection emerges. So **11 across** begins with either *low* or *law*. It has *an offer*, so *a bid* can be inserted, lightly. Ah! *law-abiding*, of course, with *to be trusted* as the definition. Let's check the rest just to be sure: *a hurry* = *a wing* (a case of misleading parts of speech) after *pound* = *l*. That's one solution that can be trusted, then.

21a Noble king pushing crown to the back (4)
The first word seems more likely to be the definition than the last. Convert the adjective *noble* to *crown* and the four-letter *earl* fits (king). *Lear's* initial letter moved to the end confirms it.

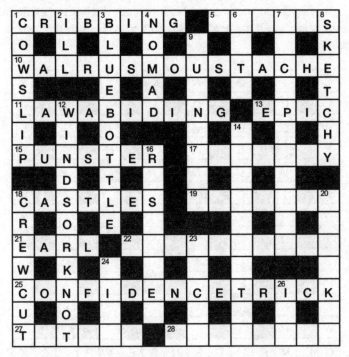

16 down proves tricky, even with friendly letters on view.

16d Male breaking his family up put on further performance (8)
Male = *m* and *family* = *kin* seem reasonably certain but what's the result? Nothing at all for now so back to the top.

6d Popular mummy beginning to undo skirt (4)
It possibly ends in *u* (*beginning to undo*) and that gives *tutu* as the *skirt*. *Mummy*, of course, is *Tut*. Why didn't I see that before?
 Earlier we failed with 5 across but now it's more straightforward:

5a Untidily throws down second pair of trousers (6)
Second can be *mo* or *s*, which fits better, getting us to *trousers* = *trews*, so there's another one cracked.

7d Is a departure so good? (11)

The second letter is likely to be *n* or *x*, and the latter leads to *exceptional*. Interesting sort of **double definition** clue as *departure* looks as if it leads to *exceptional*. However, there are *exceptionals* (non-recurring financial items) in the accounting world so that's probably it. In case it's not the explanation and hence the solution, we'll make a mental note to go back to that one if we run into trouble later.

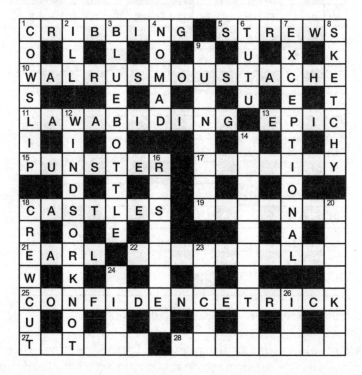

Rather stuck here, I answered a couple of e-mails before resuming.

17a Without passing judgment, peer shows uprightness (7)

That *uprightness* could be *honesty* or *probity* but neither entirely fit the wordplay. Let's see what the *p* would lead to in 9 down as that has a three-letter ending. Indeed, *mine* must be *pit* so we'll go with *probity* and a rethink.

Notice that *obit in pry* could be a **sandwich** clue with *peer = pry*. But *obit*? Presumably it refers to an obituary as a *passing judgment* so we'll also make a mental note here. Interesting that we have made good progress till these final stages but now we have some problems. That sometimes happens but we fight on.

9d Old servant becomes mine (8)

So we guessed *pit* but we're not there yet. *Becomes* could be *turns* but is a *turnspit* a *servant*? Must be one who used to cook meat for the master and a quick check with the *Concise Oxford Dictionary* (*COD*) confirms that. It's marked as a historical word which means 'still used today' as compared to archaic which means 'not in use'. Who said crosswords don't broaden the vocabulary?

19a Locker moving a nut into place when turned (7)

The words *turned*, *moving* and *into* appear to indicate a **reversal**, an **anagram** and a **sandwich**, in which case this must be a complex construction. Testing this reveals that *a nut* has to be anagrammed and put inside a reversal of *set* = *place*, so that is indeed tricky. Also, the clue has a highly misleading, some might say loose, definition of *locker* in the sense of a disease locking the jaw. Quite a challenge but we followed the components through to a conclusion without being put off by this complexity.

20d Forward one out? (7)

This has to be next and the question mark might indicate something uncertain or something unusual going on (e.g. a synonym for *forward* without *a* or *one* leading to the answer), so I was misled for a time. It's actually a **double definition** for *striker*, the punctuation presumably meaning that one such does not necessarily have to be *out* at this moment, i.e. he or she could be one who has returned to work after industrial action.

28a A kitchen device each minute pocketed by thief? (3-5)

Having briefly had another crack at the three-letter 26 down, I began to think of a break with a cuppa. That proved happy as *tea* led to *tea-maker* with *ea* = *each* plus *m* = *minute* inside *taker* = *thief* completing the **sandwich**.

23d Announcer, male, beginning to check through similar notes (5)

Here we again can work on *male* and, as it's only a five-letter solution to play with, *m* is most likely. If so that can only be the first or second letter, and the latter allows an *emcee* to announce his or her appearance. *Beginning to check* supplies the *c* and the *similar notes* must be *e*. The use of *notes* can be hard on the poor solver with any of seven possibilities (*A* to *G*) to consider but here it was no problem because the clue-writer allowed the solution to emerge first. At least, I imagine that was what was planned.

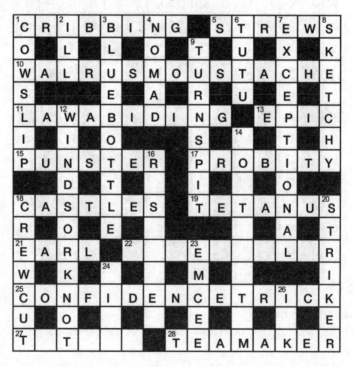

26d Like a smooth thing, doffing cap (3)

So it's either *ilk* or *ink* and, as the former is similar to *like*, I'll try to find a *smooth thing* by adding one first letter (*doffing cap*) to it. *Silk* comes to mind and confirms the answer. Not without a tiny doubt, though, as I cannot think of a sentence in which *ilk* would substitute for *like*. *Of that ilk* could hardly be *of that like* so maybe a little setter licence is being used here?

Back to 16d: Male breaking his family up put on further performance (8)

M and *kin* didn't lead anywhere so let's try the definition. Must be the last four words so *re* something and *staged* following. *Male* = *stag* then and its family is *deer* reversed outside. A very misleading, tough one.

14d One carried out when another carried off? (10)

This is the sort of clue that causes the puzzle to be abandoned, even at this stage, as it is a cryptic definition with seemingly many fields of application. As 22 across is tough too, we either take a break or resort to an electronic help (much quicker than a dictionary hunt, of course). Whatever, *postmortem* fits the bill; though note that it's unhyphenated which is probably the most common usage today. The *COD* gives it as *post-mortem* and other dictionaries

1 C	R	2 I	B	3 B	I	4 N	G	■	5 S	6 T	R	7 E	W	8 S
O	■	L	■	L	■	O	■	9 T	U	■	X	■	K
10 W	A	L	R	U	S	M	O	U	S	T	A	C	H	E
S	■	■	E	■	A	■	R	■	U	■	E	■	T
11 L	A	12 W	A	B	I	D	I	N	G	■	13 E	P	I	C
I	■	I	■	O	■	■	S	■	14 P	■	T	■	H
15 P	U	N	S	T	E	16 R	■	17 P	R	O	B	I	T	Y
■	■	D	■	T	■	E	■	I	■	S	■	O
18 C	A	S	T	L	E	S	■	19 T	E	T	A	N	U	20 S
R	■	O	■	E	■	T	■	■	M	■	A	■	T
21 E	A	R	L	■	22	A	23 E	■	O	■	L	■	R
W	■	K	■	24	■	G	■	M	■	R	■	I
25 C	O	N	F	I	D	E	N	C	E	T	R	26 I	C	K
U	■	O	■	■	D	■	E	■	E	■	L	■	E
27 T	■	T	■	■	28 T	E	A	M	A	K	E	R

as *post mortem* but *Collins English Dictionary* confirms the version here, so while being happy with that, we resist an unworthy thought that the setter could have made our task a little easier.

22a He's quick to put top hat on President's head (4-6)

Now we do have the hyphen and the split is helpful. *P* (*president's head*) must feature first, so does relating that to *ace* = *top* provide the *pace* in *he's quick*? Yes, and cricket-lovers such as your author straightaway write down *pace-bowler* and work backwards. *Hat* = *bowler*, of course, so all is present and correct with images from the clue of a speedy Jeeves in the White House quickly fading to the last two clues:

24d As a down-and-out, always be a loser? (4)
27a Design paraded? (6)

What are we to make of these clues? Very little, and this is not at all unusual at the last hurdles. 27 across may come out first with its two intersecting letters but *tatter, totter,* etc. don't seem to work. Actually there are 19 words in *COD* which would fit here (calculable from the electronic version of *COD* 11), so some lateral thinking or good old inspiration is urgently needed.

I'm pretty certain some solvers would have given up here on the basis of having more useful things to do but we are considering how to master *The Times* Crossword, so let's take another break and see whether that helps.

Yes, it does. As usual, if you can decide what type the clue is, you may be halfway there. Remember 7 down as a sort of **double definition** clue? This could be similar in that it is not two definitions side by side but one definition with allusion to another. So a cryptic definition giving *tattoo – a design* and a *parade*.

Finally 24 down: one that's not immediately apparent even with the letters. There are 26 *COD* words fitting here and the only one that is a *down-and-out* is *wino*. So the rather nice wordplay is *win nothing*, geddit?

A pleasing finale to today's endeavours and here's the whole puzzle filled in:

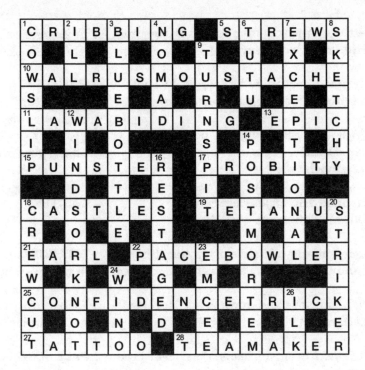

Here are the explanations, summarized. *Definitions* are in italics; <u>indicators</u> are underlined.

Across

1	After <u>first from</u> college, mocking *illicit exam technique* **Additive** including **abbreviation**	**CRIBBING** c + ribbing
5	*Untidily throws down* second pair of trousers **Additive** including **abbreviation**	**STREWS** s + trews
10	*Hairy thing*, war with USA – so much let <u>off</u> **Anagram**	**WALRUS MOUS-TACHE** (war USA so much let)*
11	Pound: an offer <u>given</u> in a hurry *to be trusted* **Additive** including **sandwich** and **abbreviation**	**LAW-ABIDING** L + a bid in a wing

13 <u>What's turned out from</u> recipes is *impressive* **Hidden** including **reversal**	**EPIC: recipes**
15 *Comedian* appears better <u>touring</u> the South **Sandwich** including **abbreviation**	**PUNSTER** s in punter
17 <u>Without</u> passing judgment, peer shows *uprightness* **Sandwich**	**PROBITY** obit in pry
18 *Men* and their *English homes?* **Double definition**	**CASTLES**
19 *Locker* <u>moving</u> a nut <u>into</u> place <u>when turned</u> **Sandwich** including **anagram** and **reversal**	**TETANUS** (a nut)* in set reversed
21 *Noble* king <u>pushing crown to the back</u> **Letter shift**	**EARL** Lear with L moved
22 *He's quick* to put top hat on President's head **Additive** including **abbreviation**	**PACE BOWLER** P + ace + bowler
25 *Deception* <u>might become</u> kind of eccentric **Anagram**	**CONFIDENCE TRICK** (kind of eccentric)*
27 *Design paraded?* **Cryptic definition**	**TATTOO**
28 *A kitchen device* each minute <u>pocketed</u> by thief? **Sandwich** including **abbreviation**	**TEA-MAKER** ea. me in taker

Down

1 One bloomer has to threaten *another* **Additive**	**COWSLIP** cow + slip
2 <u>Don't open</u> medicine, *though in need of it?* **Take away**	**ILL** pill minus p
3 Down every glug – *get a buzz out of it!* **Additive**	**BLUEBOTTLE: blue** = down + bottle

4	*Uncertain character*, though certainly not unbalanced **Additive**	**NOMAD** no + mad
6	Popular mummy <u>beginning to</u> undo *skirt* **Additive** including **abbreviation**	**TUTU** Tut + u(ndo)
7	*Is a departure so good?* **Cryptic definition**	**EXCEPTIONAL**
8	*Imprecise* score <u>written in</u> blue **Sandwich**	**SKETCHY** etch in sky
9	*Old servant* becomes mine **Additive**	**TURNSPIT** turns + pit
12	*Is one tied at royal wedding?* **Cryptic definition**	**WINDSOR KNOT**
14	*One carried out when another carried off?* **Cryptic definition**	**POSTMORTEM**
16	Male <u>breaking</u> his family <u>up</u> *put on further performance* **Sandwich** including **reversal**	**RESTAGED** stag in deer reversed
18	*Style in which redundancies effected?* **Cryptic definition**	**CREW CUT**
20	*Forward one out?* **Double definition**	**STRIKER**
23	*Announcer*, male, <u>beginning</u> to check <u>through</u> similar notes **Sandwich** including **abbreviation**	**EMCEE: m +** c(heck) in E E E
24	As *a down-and-out*, always be a loser? **Cryptic definition**	**WINO: win +** O = nothing
26	*Like* a smooth thing, <u>doffing</u> cap. **Take away**	**ILK: silk minus s**

13. From the Setter's Perspective

'I attempt yesterday's Times *crossword and manage to complete three clues – quid, Turgenev and courtier. I can only improve.'* Jeffrey Archer, *A Prison Diary – Purgatory*

In this chapter, we try to get into a setter's mind by following the process of clueing a *Times* puzzle. As is usual, the grid is prepared before clues are written.

Over to the setter:

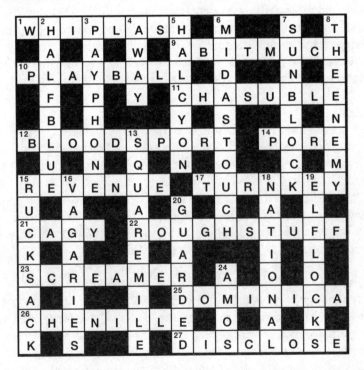

1. A setter's clueing process

When I clue a puzzle, a lot of the work is straightforward playing around with word elements, sawing and hammering at my mental workbench; but there is a moment in the creation of many clues, especially the most pleasing ones, when the elements and ideas I am working with suddenly take on a life of their own, and reassemble themselves in my brain, without any apparent conscious control on my part, into a well-constructed, often deceptive and elegant, sentence. This can happen after many minutes of fruitless cogitation, and a clue seems to hand itself to me suddenly fully-formed out of nowhere. I have no idea how or why this happens, so I have denoted these welcome moments here simply as 'Ah!'

In clueing, I like to follow Ximenes' advice, which is to start with the first clue and work through in strict order to the end. Otherwise, as he says, you are left with a few recalcitrant clues, like the hard centres in the box of chocolates that no one wants, and it takes longer to finish that way. John Sykes, the best-ever champion solver, told me that he started solving in the bottom right-hand corner, because he reckoned the compiler's brain was tired by that point and the clues were easier. Well, not every compiler goes straight through like that, but I find it the best way. So, to start at 1 across:

Whiplash:

Whiplash divides into *whip* and *lash*, two types of hit, but that is too close to the meaning of the whole word. Can *hip* be taken out somehow? It could be *hip* + *l* in *wash*; what sense can be made of that? *Hip* is bone, and *wash* is clean, which suggests a clean break of a bone – yes, *wash* can be seen as broken round *hip*. That's my idea; and a bit of work produces *Clean breaks round bone left as result of car crash*. *L/left* is a little obtrusive, but won't hurt; it is always a good idea for 1 across to be reasonably straightforward, to give the solver a good start. We can afford to get trickier as we go on!

A bit much:

This is a colloquial expression, but it is in the dictionary, so no one should object to it. *Bitch* round *mu* looks promising: *mu* is a Greek letter, a European character, and we have potentially *dog bites man* here – *A dog bit foreign character, that's not on*. Hang on: *bit* is in the answer as well as the clue, which is a weakness. Rephrase as *A dog grabbed foreign character, that's not on*.

Play ball:

A double definition should work here, using the literal and metaphorical meanings of the phrase – to kick a ball around, and to cooperate. It needs phrasing to make the construction less obvious, so one definition slightly more allusive: *Boys love to cooperate* – not so obvious that *Boys love to* is a definition. Sexist these days singling out boys rather than girls? Well, actually it's not strictly true anyway – so let's make it *Most boys love to cooperate*.

Chasuble:
I put this word in, thinking to refer to Canon Chasuble in Wilde's *Importance of Being Earnest*, but have had second thoughts, as it is a minor role and may not be familiar enough. Nor, perhaps, might the other meaning, a priest's vestment at Eucharist. Maybe an anagram? *Clubs*, *a* and *he* may be some useful raw material. A smashing club? Breaking a club (over one's knee, having missed a putt)? The suit of clubs? I will see what links best with the definition: and how to word this? *Vestment* is boring; what of the context? Ah! One wears it for liturgical celebration, and one can celebrate in a club – and do some damage to it. *Trashing a club he's celebrated in* is nearly there: the definition needs to lead accurately to the noun answer. A little thought produces *A club he's trashed that one is celebrating in*.

Blood sport:
Claret used to be a slang term for blood, so *claret* and *port* look like a good start; we need to weave in the *s* and find a definition that goes with the sense. *Claret succeeded by fortified wine* ... a second drink may be a *chaser*: can we work this into the definition, thinking of hunting? Maybe it is not close enough; there are other chases that aren't blood-sports – steeple-chasing, drag hunting, etc. Some thought suggests 'A deadly pursuit' as the definition, much stronger and more accurate, and arguably reasonable in the context of foolish drinking. On review, I see I used *succeeded* for *s* in another clue (*sunblock*). I don't like using an abbreviation twice in one puzzle, so I rework this to *Following claret with second, stronger wine is a deadly pursuit*.

Pore:
I was thinking of a homophone clue here (sounds like *pour*), but am not sure the pronunciation of these words is equivalent all round the country, so it would be safer to avoid it. The word has a number of meanings, so I can make a double definition: *Gaze in small opening*. No, that's not quite right: gaze (at) is not exactly equivalent to pore (over). Instead, then, *Look intently in small opening*.

Revenue:
This cries out for *even* inside *rue*, as we haven't had a sandwich clue yet. *Rue* is a herb, or to regret; neither has an obvious association with meanings of *revenue* – income, earnings. *Holding steady, regret income?* Doesn't make any sense. Ah! We could refer to a *revenue stream: stream* will fit the sense better. *Stream, perhaps* (as it is not a definition of a stream) *runs smooth through (pieces of) herb* should be workable into a neat sentence: eventually come up with *With herb banks, smooth stream perhaps*.

Turnkey:
An old word for jailer, one who locks you up: so *locker* can make a deceptive definition. Given that, the wordplay can afford to be simple: so *n* in *turkey* looks good. The result is *Plan finally to partition country found in old locker*.

Cagy:
This word, an alternative spelling of *cagey*, doesn't break down into anything, so some deceptive definitions are needed. Cages have bars; a pun on bar? *Like bars, giving nothing away.* Not terribly brilliant, but I can't think of anything better.

Rough stuff:
These words rhyme, which can often furnish a theme for a clue; but my hopes of marrying that with a definition to make anything interesting came to nothing. Word analysis doesn't look hopeful either: there is *s* in *ought* in *ruff*, but that is going to get over-complicated. Perhaps an anagram? *Fought* is in there, which is related to the meaning, always a promising avenue. Taking out *fought* leaves *rsuf*, which fortunately makes a word – *furs*. So *In furs, fought violently* for the wordplay, and this seems to lead to the answer in itself, which is a bonus: *In furs, fought violently – the result?*

Screamer:
Screamer is a publisher's term for an exclamation mark, which would make a wonderfully deceptive definition. So I only have to look for some wordplay that could justify the mark at the end: there is *cr* in *seamer: Bowler receives credit*, but why should that be an exclamation? An alternative is *s* + *creamer* – *s* on its own again, which must have a different treatment from the other *ss*. *First to spurn powdered milk!* (*First, opening, last, finally* are very helpful aids for extracting virtually any otherwise-recalcitrant letter; one must be careful to use them sparingly.)

Dominica:
I have often seen this word in puzzles, but have only just thought that it is *do* plus most of *minicab*. So: *Make taxi drop one off in the country*. Perhaps *one off* isn't specific enough about which letter to drop, so I refine this to *Make taxi drop last one off in the country*. (The ever-nagging need to balance conciseness, smoothness, fairness and solvability.)

Chenille:
When I put this word in, I noticed it was an anagram of *Hellenic*, and one-word anagrams are nice, since they are often not too obvious. A simple matter to write down *Hellenic woven cloth*.

Disclose:
Dis- is a cliché element – *dis* = *hell*, *di's* = *girl's*; avoid if at all possible. An anagram? *Sold ices? Do slices?* Doesn't look very interesting. Back to the original idea of *dis/close*: with *close* = *near*, pronounced differently from the *-close* in *disclose*, this could be sufficiently misleading, and a bit of work produces a nice surface meaning in *Announce daughter is about to arrive*. Not hard, but that is less important than accuracy and elegance.

Now for the down clues.

Half-blue:
This looks a promising word – *turquoise* (blue/green) could be one definition, and the player of a minor university sport the other. Riding (horses) turns out to be such a sport; especially useful as any references to riding/riders may mislead the experienced solver into expecting the cliché *up* to appear somewhere. What about *Rider perhaps in turquoise?* Nice surface meaning, since jockeys wear colours, but doubts are nagging me: riding as a half-blue won't be familiar, and *turquoise* is maybe a little tendentious as a definition. I think one element of the clue at least must be more helpful, so reluctantly I will change this to *Rider perhaps gets a little beer down*. This will be easily solved, but it is fairer, which is the crucial point; and there will be difficulty enough elsewhere in the puzzle.

Pay-phone:
This word doesn't analyse easily, but I thought of a nice deceptive definition: *Calls here for coins*. Only, on reviewing the clues later, I see this is neither a good definition, nor does it make a lot of sense. Why on earth did I put that down? Now I see *one* on the end: so, at the cost of an anagram, we could have

Stupidly happy person ... but how to fit in a definition? Is *coins* right, or are there only cards these days? Ringing? Ringer? Ah! Coins for a ring, for someone getting engaged (cheaply, if it's only coins!) – who should be deliriously happy. So: *Deliriously happy person offering coins for a ring here.*

Away:

I clue this word a lot (*A-A-* being a common sequence of letters in a grid) and have some trouble thinking of a new idea. We haven't used a hidden clue yet, and this may be the place for it. I want to use the definition *off*, which may look like part of the wordplay; and the trickiest bit is to find an indicator that isn't too obvious (*inside*, *part of* won't make solvers think for more than a second). *A year off* is promising sense; how to add the *aw* on the front? Ah! *Offered by law a year off* does the trick.

Halcyon:

The kingfisher, and a mythical bird which charmed nature into stillness – hence halcyon days, a period of serenity, probably the only use of this word nowadays. My definition will be one out of *calm*, *serene*, *undisturbed*; but the word analysis is not easy, and it occurs to me that the disturbance of an anagram (*any loch*; *can holy*) wouldn't make good surface sense. Why did I put this word in! Eventually, decide on a technique of hiding the word in alternate letters: *-lcy-* offers *lucky*, then good sense is *lucky wound is undisturbed*, and the *ha* could be *heal*. I need an indicator for the technique; nothing seamless comes to mind, and I can't do better than with *Regularly heal: lucky wound is undisturbed*. The rest of the clue is OK, though.

Midas touch:

There are lots of anagram possibilities here: *it's much ado, I had custom*; but I can't see a sensible context to put these into. What about breaking the solution into pieces? *I'd* in *mast* plus *ouch*? Not much sense there either! Two-word expressions are often good for double definitions, especially when there is a literal and a common meaning; and it is good to mix up the clue types, and not make all the clues out of jigsaw bits and pieces. Midas's touch turned things literally to gold, in the Greek myth, so he had *valuable contacts*, and the modern meaning is the lucky break, or a run of good fortune, so I'll try *Lucky art of making valuable contacts*. (The word *lucky* now appears in consecutive clues, doing different work each time. Stylistically, is this good or bad? Don't know!)

Sunblock:

S plus *unblock* looks promising here. *Free* would be nice for *unblock*, as it can fit into a clue in so many ways. Sunblock protects the skin, suggesting *saving one's skin, scot-free*, as a theme for the surface meaning. Taking *succeeded* as one of the uses of the letter *s* (does anyone use this outside crosswords?), I end up with *Succeeded getting free – that's to save one's skin*.

The enemy:

A phrase used jocularly for *time*, so a simple double definition, but some work needed to find a simple formulation: *Time not for us?* No; the normal word order is *Not time for us*, which doesn't work. *Time is against us?* That might work, but it seems more like a straight definition. Finally decide on *Time to fight*.

Square mile:

The City of London, so *city* is a precise definition that doesn't give too much away; but it needs really a capital *C*, which means it has to be the first word of the clue. *Qu* is an awkward combination to play with; and the word doesn't seem to break down easily, other than into its two actual words, which I always think a weakness. We haven't had too many anagrams yet; a little searching produces *equaliser*, which I haven't seen used before, but with the *m* left over. *Equaliser* and *City* looks a promising football context. We need an anagram indicator: *unusual, unexpected*? Neither word is strong enough to indicate the disturbance of an anagram, for me; but *scrambled equaliser for City* makes good sense, and neatly solves the initial-capital problem. What about the *m*? Ah! We can extend the anagram nicely into *Scrambled equaliser, first for Manchester City*. Pedants could argue the definition should be *the* City, but I am pleased with that one!

Rucksack:

A simple additive clue – *Fight and plunder carrier*. Reasonably deceptive sense, and nice and quick to create.

Vagaries:

Vagaries are unexpected changes; *Aries* is an astrological sign; what to do with *vag*? *G* stands for *good*, so *a/g/aries* would look nice as *a good sign* – leaving the *v* to deal with. *V* can stand for *velocity*, and *changes in velocity* makes good sense, especially as the solver would tend to read it as a single phrase, instead of as part of the definition plus a bit of wordplay – that would be nice deception. Putting that together makes *Unexpected changes in velocity a good sign*. For sense, it might be better if they were *not* a good sign; but I can't work that in, and it will be fine as it is.

National:

Often clued as a double definition, with reference to the Grand National; and not easy to find a new treatment. The word is only one letter different from *rational*, the difference being the *head*, always easy to refer to; so the elements will be *countryman* and *logical*, with *n* instead of *r*. *R = river* would fit the country sense; so, *Countryman using logic has name for river* – and we didn't need to use *head* after all.

Elf-locks:

This means *matted hair*. *Flocks* leaps out of this, with the image of sheep with tangled coats; but how to handle *el*? *The Spanish* is boring, and doesn't add to the image. Ah! Coats can mean *covers, goes round*, so if we have a single flock then *ELS coats* it: *sheep in ELS coats have tangled fleece*. *ELS* looks like *ELS(E)*, a short *else* – now we can work up a nice contrast between long, tangled wool and something short. *A tangled mop, some sheep – otherwise short coats* does it. (No verb in this sentence, so one could say it was a bit *clipped*!)

Guarded:

This means *cagy*, so we could cross-refer to 21 across; but it occurs to me that the double definition clue *Reticent with escort* would be nice, because *with escort* doesn't look like a definition at first sight.

Amos:

The last one! Very easy to analyse this word in any number of ways, but I am not going to try to be too clever. *Amos* is a book in the Bible, so defining A as (the indefinite) article will make a good sense link: *Article doctor's put into book*.

All done; with breaks, a full day's work. It looks OK, with a good selection of clue types, including four anagrams and one hidden clue. Tomorrow, I will look over it, type it up, check the answer lengths, spelling, etc., and scan the clues for any obvious mistakes. Then it goes away in the drawer, to be looked at again with a fresh eye before it goes to *The Times*.

   Opposite is the finished result, with definitions in italics and indicators underlined.

2. The final clues from the setter's clueing process

(*Definitions* are in italics, <u>indicators</u> are underlined.)

Across

1 Clean breaks <u>round</u> bone left as *a result of car crash* (8)
Sandwich
WHIPLASH – hip + l in wash

9 A dog <u>grabbed</u> foreign character? That's *not on* (1,3,4)
Sandwich
A BIT MUCH – mu in a bitch

10 *Most boys love to cooperate* (4,4)
Double definition
PLAY BALL

11 A club he's <u>trashed</u>, *that one is celebrating in* (8)
Anagram
CHASUBLE – a club he's*

12 Following claret with second, stronger wine is a *deadly pursuit* (5,5)
Additive
BLOOD SPORT – blood + s + port

14 *Look intently in small opening* (4)
Double definition
PORE

15 <u>With</u> herb <u>banks</u>, smooth *stream perhaps* (7)
Sandwich
REVENUE – even in rue

17 Plan finally <u>to partition</u> country found in *old locker* (7)
Sandwich
TURNKEY – n in Turkey

21 *Like bars giving little away* (4)
Double definition
CAGY

22 In furs, fought <u>violently</u> – *the result?* (5,5)
Anagram
ROUGH STUFF – furs fought*

23 First to spurn powdered milk! (8)
Additive
SCREAMER (= exclamation mark) – s + creamer

25 Make taxi <u>drop</u> last one off in *the country* (8)
Additive including **take away**
DOMINICA – do + minica(b)

26 Hellenic <u>woven</u> *cloth* (8)
Anagram
CHENILLE – Hellenic*

27 *Announce* daughter's about to arrive (8)
Additive
DISCLOSE – d is close

Down

2 *Rider perhaps* gets a little beer down (4-4)
Additive
HALF-BLUE – half + blue

3 <u>Deliriously</u> happy person offering *coins for a ring here* (3-5)
Anagram
PAY-PHONE – happy* + one

4 <u>Offered by</u> law a year *off* (4)
Hidden
AWAY – law a year

5 <u>Regularly</u> heal: lucky wound is *undisturbed* (7)
Anagram
HALYCON – h(e)a(l) l(u)c(k)y (w)o(u)n(d)

6 *Lucky art of making valuable contacts* (5,5)
Cryptic definition
MIDAS TOUCH

7 Succeeded getting free – *that's to save one's skin* (8)
Additive
SUNBLOCK – s + unblock

8 *Time to fight* (3,5)
Cryptic definition
THE ENEMY

13 Scrambled equaliser first for Manchester *City* (6,4)
Anagram
SQUARE MILE – equaliser M*

15 Fight and plunder *carrier* (8)
Additive
RUCKSACK – ruck + sack

16 *Unexplained changes* in velocity a good sign (8)
Additive
VAGARIES – v + a g Aries

18 *Countryman* using logic has name for river (8)
Letter switch
NATIONAL – rational with N for R

19 *A tangled mop*, some sheep – otherwise short coats (3,5)
Sandwich
ELF-LOCKS – flock in els(e)

20 *Reticent with escort* (7)
Double definition
GUARDED

24 Article doctor's put into *book* (4)
Additive
AMOS – A + MO's

14: Raising Your Game

> '*Come into the library and we'll do* The Times *together.*'
> '*You have the oddest idea of relaxation.*'
> Noël Coward, *Brief Encounter*

We will now look at methods that you might consider for improving your crossword-solving skills for *The Times* Crossword.

1. Practice, practice, practice!
This is the number one recommendation for improvement. There are many verbal tricks and conventions that are more easily recognized after you have done lots of crosswords. That still leaves room for setters to provide new ones, so have no fear that boredom will set in! You may like to practise by trying some of the clues and puzzles later in the book.

2. Solve with a friend
People often tell me that they enjoy doing all or part of the puzzle with a family member or work colleague. This can be face-to-face, via phone, text or email and the resultant interchanges seem to lead to a speeding-up of the learning process. One of my recent workshop groups has formed an internet-based cooperation to help each other solve and to keep in touch on crossword matters.

3. Join The Times Online Crossword Club
Go to **www.timesonline.co.uk/crossword**
   For a relatively small annual sum, you can join this community of *Times* Crossword lovers. It contains current and archive puzzles with solutions (though not to that day's puzzles, of course) for crosswords such as these:

The Times Cryptic	**Times Sports**
Times Jumbo	**Sunday Times Cryptic**
Times 2	**Sunday Times Mephisto**
Times 2 Jumbo	**Times Literary Supplement**

As well a bulletin board, competitions and puzzles set exclusively for *Times Online*, there is a monthly clue-writing contest. The archive dates back to 2000 and if you need more practice to make perfect, this could be the site for you.

4. Buy a *Times* book of puzzles

If good old-fashioned books are what you prefer, then one of the HarperCollins *Times* books may appeal. There are books for most of the puzzles mentioned on the previous page. Some discipline is of course needed as the solutions in the back are all too readily accessible before completion.

5. Enjoy a crossword workshop

Strictly not competitive and open to all, whatever your existing standard, a crossword workshop is a fun way to improve. Details of those perhaps coming up in your area are available on various websites, including the author's:

www.timmoorey.info

www.mcsummerschool.org.uk

www.earnley.co.uk

www.farncombeestate.co.uk

www.conferencecentrewales.co.uk

www.womens-institute.co.uk

6. Watch the annual *Times* Crossword Competition

I imagine that seeing others solve in amazingly quick times could be soul-destroying but perhaps a total immersion for one day in *The Times* Crossword, with the possibility of exchanges with like-minded people, contestants and spectators, could be useful.

7. Join a Crossword Club

The Crossword Club, Awbridge, Hampshire: **www.thecrosswordclub.co.uk**
  For the past thirty years, this club run by Brian Head has published a monthly magazine (both printed and electronic versions) with puzzles, articles and competitions. It also offers an agony aunt (the Cluru) for clue solution explanations that have defeated you.

The Australian Crossword Club is similar and can be found at **www.crosswordclub.org**

8. Study the published solutions

Though explanations are not published, it can be highly productive to study the solutions published and to work backwards for any clues you have not managed to crack the previous day (or days, in the case of weekends). I believe many would like to see annotated solutions but space limitations prevail.

PART 3

PRACTICE TIME

15: Recommended Books, Electronic Aids and Websites

'What a comfort a dictionary is!' Lewis Carroll, *Sylvie and Bruno*

There's much more help available than just a dictionary these days. In fact an increasing number of books, websites and electronic gadgets offer assistance as well as crosswords. Here are some recommendations:

Specifically for *The Times* Crossword

1. Dictionaries
All words and phrases used in *The Times* Crossword are justifiable by reference to a dictionary or other major reference book, normally the bold type entries therein. The principal dictionaries used by *Times* setters are the latest versions of *Collins English Dictionary* and the *Concise Oxford Dictionary*. If the meaning of a word is in neither, the most likely explanation is that it is a new usage. Note that in recent and current editions, Collins has omitted names of people (*Bonn* is there but not *Beethoven*) though you will find both in *Collins English Dictionary PRO*, an online dictionary at **www.collinslanguage.com**
The *Chambers Biographical Dictionary* is one way of filling this gap.

2. Thesauruses
Collins, Oxford and Chambers all publish useful dictionaries of synonyms and all three are more efficient for crossword solvers than the longer established *Roget's Thesaurus*, whose use can involve lots of page-turning for any one reference.

3. Word list books
Collins Bradford's Crossword Solver's Dictionary, 7th Edition:
This has been the book of choice among crossword cognoscenti for over twenty years, principally because of its method of production. Not having been compiled from computerized lists, it was, and continues to be, built up

by its author, Anne Bradford, from solutions actually appearing in a variety of crosswords including *The Times* Crossword. That means you have a good chance of finding the name of, say, that elusive horse (well over 200 entries) to complete the puzzle.

Chambers Crossword Dictionary, 2nd Edition:

This is a relative newcomer which nicely complements *Bradford's*. The Chambers book features many lists of anagrams and other indicators, plus articles thereon. It is rare for a word in the *Times* not to be found in one or other of these two books, both of which are published in cheaper, pocket-sized editions.

4. Electronic aids
Pocket machines:

Sharp PWE300 or 500A
This includes the *Oxford Dictionary*, the *Oxford Thesaurus* and, in the case of the PWE500A, the *Oxford Dictionary of Quotations*, all searchable by individual words and phrases. Like the pocket machine recommended next, it has anagram and Wordsearch facilities. Thus, if you need to find a four-letter word ending in *j* you will do so easily and quickly. I have used the PWE500 (now PWE500A) for several years instead of carrying dictionaries and wordlist books around.

Bradford's Crossword Solver CSB-1470
A more recent arrival for serious crossword fans, this has a cut-down (although still pretty useful) version of *Bradford's Crossword Solver's Dictionary* as well as many other features, even including an encyclopaedia with proper names. Though not as user-friendly as the Sharp, it is probably the most useful of the large Franklin range of electronic aids for solvers.

Software for Handhelds and Smartphones
As well as many downloadable dictionaries and thesauruses from, say, Oxford and Merriam-Webster, there is a very basic but effective Palm-based program called AardWord that contains Wordsearch using a very large wordbase with many obscure words that appear in Chambers' and Collins' dictionaries. It also makes light work of whole-word anagrams.

5. Websites
Times Online Crossword Club at www.timesonline.co.uk/crossword:
See Chapter 14 for details on this wonderful resource for *Times* Crossword lovers.

Dictionaries:
If you don't have one of the electronic aids listed above, and are in the mood for a spot of 'cheating', Collins, Oxford and Chambers all have Wordsearch facilities online, as well as some of their dictionaries.

For reference, Wikipedia:
For all its well-reported weaknesses in terms of reliability, its comprehensiveness makes it a first choice if you want a quick check on a factual solution.

6. Blogs: online crossword discussion
One excellent place in the blogosphere for comment on each day's puzzle is:

Times for the Times:
http://community.livejournal.com/times_xwd_times
This has a blog (a daily journal) which includes solving times, highlighting of good clues and tricky points about each *Times* puzzle. Its expressed aims are:

- To assess the difficulty and quality of puzzles
- To help new (and sometimes experienced) solvers understand how the more difficult clues work
- To provide a place where solvers (and some setters) of *The Times* Crossword and other crosswords can exchange views by adding comments.

A panel of bloggers (led by champion solver Peter Biddlecombe, who does an excellent job) provides the initial commentary to which additional comments are made by keen *Times* solvers. Most bloggers are faster than average and some are phenomenally quick; comments such as 'Time taken today: 4 min 25 secs which would have been less had I not entered a wrong solution at 26 across,' are not unusual.

As yet, setters seem only occasionally to enter into the discussion but maybe their participation will increase. As a setter finding my puzzles blogged is useful feedback on what's liked and disliked though I have to keep in mind that the site is manned by those in the upper echelons of the crossword world.

7. *Times* Crossword history

75 Years of the Times Crossword, published by Collins in 2005, has puzzles from the very first to modern times. With a foreword by regular *Times* solver, Colin Dexter, it sets many of its 75 crosswords in a historical context.

8. Books of *Times* Crosswords

These are the most recently published:

- *The Times Crossword Book 12*, edited by Richard Browne
- *The Times Jumbo Cryptic Crosswords Book 8*
- *The Times T2 Book 12*, edited by John Grimshaw
- *The Times Listener Crosswords 2008*

For other crosswords

1. Dictionaries

Chambers Dictionary (11th edition 2008), though not officially on *The Times* list, is the standard recommendation for the most advanced puzzles such as the *Times Listener* Crossword, Mephisto (*Sunday Times*) and Azed (*Observer*). Containing many humorous definitions, rare words and Scotticisms, it's a valuable, entertaining and idiosyncratic resource as many word lovers know.

> **DID YOU KNOW?**
> One crossword setter in the 1960s, wishing to include the word *miniskirts* in a puzzle, found that the word had not yet been added to the *Chambers Dictionary*, and came up with the wonderful clue:
>
> *They should not be looked up in Chambers Dictionary.*

2. Websites

The most comprehensive site for solvers of the *Times* and crosswords of a similar standard is run by Derek Harrison in his The Crossword Centre at **www.crossword.org.uk**. It has an especially lively and interesting message board which discusses crosswords from many different sources, including *The Times*. Most commonly there are discussions and comments on *The Times Listener* Crossword which has its own comprehensive website at **www.listenercrossword.com**

3. Crossword manual
The Chambers Crossword Manual by Don Manley covers the crossword field comprehensively and authoritatively and is now in its fourth edition. It is especially strong on outlining and recommending the principles of Ximenes, as compared to what author and champion clue-writer, Colin Dexter, in a book review in *The Oldie* magazine, has called 'libertarian' crossword principles.

4. Ultimate authority: Ximenes
For the horse's mouth on this aspect and lessons in setting, Derrick Macnutt's *Ximenes on the Art of the Crossword*, published first in 1966 and reprinted in 2001, is a book to enjoy. Not only witty and elegant, it includes ten puzzles by famed setters Torquemada, Afrit and Ximenes himself. As Derek Harrison has commented: 'This is far more than a treatise, it's thought-provoking and a pleasure to read.'

5. Insights into anonymous setters
Finally, if you want to discover who lurks behind the curious pseudonyms used by setters (though not of course the *Times*'s), try the *A–Z of Crosswords* by Ximenes' successor Azed, Jonathan Crowther. Published in 2006, it contains puzzles chosen by many setters themselves as best representing their work.

16: Clues and Puzzles for Practice

'He tried to concentrate on the black and white squares. He wasn't very good at crosswords. "Grebe reared in Northern Scandinavian city (6)". He liked anagrams best. Little rearrangements. "Bergen."'
Kate Atkinson, *One Good Turn*

The clues and puzzles used for demonstration and practice have all appeared in *The Times*. They are selected because I enjoyed them and I believe they are good representatives of *The Times* Crossword. After you have studied this book, my hope is that you will be surprised by how many puzzles you are able to solve with only a little or no 'cheating'. Many may seem intractable on first glance but please do not be put off – some of them appeared intractable to me as well.

1. Clues to try

You may wish to improve your solving skills by tackling these clues first. I have chosen them as excellent examples of the most enjoyable aspects of *The Times* Crossword and, in a very few cases, elsewhere in cryptic crosswords. Many of them were selected as 'Clue of the Week', a feature of *The Week* magazine over the past ten years in which the best clue from any source is published. *The Times* has featured more than any other newspaper or magazine in 'Clue of the Week'.

The first five in each set of clues offer a little extra help and, as before, indicators are underlined in clue types which contain them. The solutions to these Clues to Try are in the Appendices, starting on page 189.

See solutions on pages 189-190

ANAGRAM CLUES

1. Adhesive tapes <u>come unstuck</u> (5, first letter P)
2. One could claim <u>damages</u> à la rugby (8, first letter A)
3. It's a crime <u>breaking</u> a truce (9, first letter A)
4. Need AGM <u>arranged</u> close to board meeting (7, first letter E)
5. Gee – Old Glory <u>ill befits</u> British PM! (5,6, first letters L and G)
6. Anti-abortionist fixed it for the girl (5-2-5)
7. Tip of offensive hardware being shot (9)
8. Old man takes violin to play in summerhouse (8)
9. International meetings – often scenic summer thrashes? (6,11)
10. Break down after moving letters from close pal (8)

SANDWICH CLUES

1. Shock seeing *Times* leader <u>in</u> unlikely location (4, first letter S)
2. It may make us take shelter <u>in</u> centre of Boston (5, first letter S)
3. Scrap copper <u>collected by</u> motor sport bodies (10, first letter F)
4. Lacking the will <u>to cross</u> river between parts of US (10, first letter I)
5. Time <u>in</u> cell? But one isn't charged (7, first letter N)
6. Left tart after eating slice of apple and cheese (4,5)
7. Go on bed inside which there's a rat! (8)
8. Incy Wincy Spider, say, caught in rain, had gone up the spout (8)
9. Hunt the writer in a way that's cunning (7)
10. Indigestion? A most troubled hour in store! (7,4)

TAKE AWAY CLUES

1. It's better <u>avoided by</u> one renouncing alcohol (4, first letter B)
2. Enthusiastic call from people <u>losing</u> head and heart (6, first letter E)
3. <u>No</u> time for nurse's work – that's final! (6, first letter E)
4. Old scientist agreed to cut a holiday <u>short</u> (10, first letter A)
5. Singer in state of nudity? Get her <u>off</u>! (4, first letter A)
6. Perhaps unwisely hospital's gone private (6)
7. First off most harsh mountain (7)
8. Administrators are at heart grey men (7)
9. Take tip from champion craftsman (7)
10. Perhaps a lorry needs empty lane (7)

See solutions on pages 190-192

LETTER SWITCH CLUES

1   Source of inspiration to preach 'the first shall be last and...' (5, first letter E)
2   What is replacing a tricky contest? (5, first letter W)
3   Queen of France has replaced one divine female (5, first letter I)
4   Do a heart transplant for Tom (5, first letter C)
5   Fish moves south along the coast (3,5, first letters S and H)
6   Resigned after editor's move to change structure (8)
7   Change of direction at end of dangerous river (6)
8   Struggled getting roast out of one oven into another (6)

REVERSAL CLUES

1   At short notice, send back information (4, first letter D)
2   Indian governor sent back in run out (5, first letter N)
3   After retirement, go round the bend (4, first letter B)
4   Save from boat capsizing (3, a down clue, first letter T)
5   Given money back on return of this napkin (6, first letter D)
6   Fabric that's the reverse of a bargain – rubbish! (9)
7   Revealing material writer turned up (5, a down clue)
8   Ties up this turf (5, a down clue)
9   Did some work at last, having turned up in Greek Island (5, a down clue)
10   Huge flans all round – that's the trick! (9)

HIDDEN CLUES

1   Swimmer turning in special pool (6, first letter P)
2   Slight item coming between raisin and sultana (6, first letter I)
3   Mount Vesuvius strikes, engulfing Naples, taking just seconds (4, first letter E)
4   Some unceremonious language (5, first letter S)
5   Novel penned by Alessandro Manzoni (5, first letter R)
6   Roof space full of these boxes (4)
7   Sensation concealed by Chopin, Sand needlessly (4,3,7)
8   Some job at hand? We'll soon see (4,3,5)
9   She's repeatedly kept in bed - it helped, I think (5)
10   Happy perhaps being involved in battlefield warfare (5)

See solutions on pages 192-193

HOMOPHONE CLUES

1 <u>Part</u> of the church where one hears 'I will' (5, first letter A)
2 Man's <u>spoken of</u> busy junction (5, first letter C)
3 <u>Sound</u> battery to dispose of (4, first letter S)
4 Taken in school – <u>oral</u> (5, first letter E)
5 Composer close to Britten <u>in sound</u> (7, first letter I)
6 Planet revolved rapidly, we hear (5)
7 Courtiers heard building fences (9)
8 Green space to disappear, it's said – stop using the car! (4,4)
9 Superior sort of busybody, say (5)
10 Weapon in front of ship? Doesn't sound like it (3)

ALL-IN-ONE CLUES

1 Who carried the can, losing head <u>sadly</u>? (9,6, first letters C and H)
2 <u>What could</u> be the last course? That's <u>about</u> right (9,5, first letters C and R)
3 A nit is often <u>the product of this</u> (11, first letter I)
4 Real patriots <u>after revolution</u>? (12, first letter P)
5 Time we have <u>to hold</u> start of lunch (6, first letter T)
6 Reverse of fine and cool (4)
7 Hood's resort few disturbed (8,6)
8 Fantastic crowd puller? Not half! (5,3)
9 Is a bit less wobbly (10)
10 Activity of person hanging round races? (7)

DOUBLE DEFINITION CLUES

1 Try Morse (9, first letter E)
2 Units working for the queen (4, first letter O)
3 House team (5, first letter V)
4 Fully extended, eventually (2,6, first letters A and L)
5 Sound like hounds, or one of the horses (3, first letter B)
6 Punishment that ends with a period in the US (8)
7 Fail to fill out Conference form? (2,4-6)
8 Made out to be important (13)
9 Psychiatrist's contract (6)
10 Detached supplement to a will (4)

See solutions on pages 193-195

CRYPTIC DEFINITION CLUES

1 Stored in it all the letters one writes (8, first letter A)
2 Beat with hands raised? (7, first letter O)
3 Sheet anchor (11, first letter P)
4 It may be said to limit one's drinking supply (4, first letter W)
5 They check wheels on their watches that have stopped (7,7, first letters T and W)
6 Mug presented at christening? (4-4)
7 What's said to make controversy controversial? (13)
8 Poles are put down by these Italians (10)
9 Men that are sometimes moved to mate (5,6)
10 Runs out of gas? (6,9)

ADDITIVE CLUES

1 Development of fine photograph (8, first letter O)
2 Married to a Northerner - lucky thing! (6, first letter M)
3 Vegetable presented with a dessert? That's a bloomer (5,3, first letters S and P)
4 FA present head of training (4, first letter N)
5 Bird left safe haven during flood (4, first letter L)
6 Rented holiday home in very bad area (5)
7 Dessert wines no great shakes (11)
8 Son having Indian food gets runs (8)
9 Hollywood's location causing a sensation all the time (9)
10 Wine-merchant's opening branches for Christmas in every area (6)

NOVELTY CLUES

1 Inappropriate comment of rugby player meeting queen (8, first letter I)
2 Pieces of chintz are ordered in this way - for wool it's the opposite (10, first letter A)
3 Show dogs and horses (5-2-8, first letter P)
4 I can identify vehicles from here (5, first letter I)
5 Appropriate payments for Henry James and Edward Lear? (9, first letter R)
6 The tube fare (2,6)
7 Uproar caused by one line getting shifted in Europe's capitals (6)
8 Computer program suggesting neccesary changes? (12)
9 Has had, for example, to make a change in this (5)
10 If one cold toe is numb, two must be _____ (4,6)

2. Complete the clue

Some find that they are able to solve clues more easily once they get themselves in the mind of the setter. These next 30 clues have a single word missing and the idea is that you need to become the setter rather than solver to complete the clue. The figures in brackets are the lengths of the missing words and, in some cases, the first letter of the answer is given. See page 195 for the missing words.

	COMPLETE THE CLUE	SOLUTION
1	How long will you ___? (2)	LIFESPAN
2	_____ loser? Ridiculous! (4)	ROOSEVELT
3	Root out _____ of problem, and then do it again (5) *First letter of answer is H*	OBLITERATE
4	Extreme break-out _____ guards (9) *First letter of answer is T*	UTTER
5	SAD ain't _____? Could be this worked? (7)	ANTI-DEPRESSANT
6	What may show reduced waist measurement _____ to exercise? (6)	TAPE
7	He looks as if he hasn't washed the back of his _____ (4)	SCRUFF
8	_____ cricket is no diversion for boffin (4)	ROCKET SCIENTIST
9	Complaint of plane passenger that may involve the handling of _____ (4) *First letter of answer is B*	AIRSICKNESS
10	Soldiers could make a military _____ crossing end of desert (5)	TERRITORIAL ARMY
11	Instructions for enjoying cigarette at _____ of day (5)	FIRST LIGHT
12	Where there may be a requirement for prior expertise, _____ inside (7) *First letter of answer is W*	MONASTERY
13	_____ lifers to stir for solitary (4)	FRIENDLESS
14	Theatre _____ possibly drawing in millions (4)	THE MOUSE TRAP
15	These _____ one's sort (4) *First letter of answer is F*	THE LIKES OF

16	A drier's ___ when working (4)	**HAIRDRESSER**
17	_____ woman of ill-repute getting pulled at Northern club (7) *First letter of answer is T*	**LUTON TOWN**
18	A chap could attend this celebration but never ___ (4) *First letter of answer is D*	**STAG PARTY**
19	Great Dane is _____ in open-air restaurant (7) *First letter of answer is B*	**TEA GARDEN**
20	Square _____ is bowler's target (3)	**NINEPIN**
21	One way to get ___ relaxed (4) *First letter of answer is F*	**LAIDBACK**
22	Meal eaten ___ (2)	**HIGH TEA**
23	_____ - place in which there's quiet estate, perhaps (6) *First letter of answer is B*	**PUSHCART**
24	_____ firm leaving barrister to seek information (8) *First letter of answer is G*	**UNSELFISH**
25	Something over my _____- with no end of puzzlement, I finally get it! (4)	**AHA**
26	Riots ruined most of course! It makes you ____! (4)	**ROTISSERIE**
27	Poetic device exemplified in Keats and ____ (5)	**EYE-RHYME**
28	Who might show a sort of elitist _____? (7)	**INTELLIGENTSIA**
29	River in old _____ turned out an apt place to live (4)	**HOUSEBOAT**
30	_____ blocking account receives backing (6) *First letter of answer is B*	**CERT**

3. Puzzles to try

Extra help is given for the first puzzle, starting overleaf; the rest are as printed originally. There are comprehensive notes with each solution (see page 197). Studying these carefully should be rewarding for many readers. To minimize page-turning, the clues are repeated with the notes.

The order in which the puzzles appear bears some resemblance to their level of difficulty, though undoubtedly not everyone will agree on these levels.

Practice Puzzle 1:
(Clues have definitions in italics and clue type given in bold afterwards.)

Across

2 *Calm down*, if breaking fast (6)
  Sandwich
4 One medicine briefly held back in *large-scale health emergency* (8)
  Sandwich including **reversal** and **abbreviation**
10 *Fruit* pie, originally, cooked with last pear (4-5)
  Anagram including **abbreviation**
11 *Device* of American providing private health care? (5)
  Novelty
12 *For Japanese ceremony, leaves much to be desired?* (3)
  Cryptic definition
13 *Fiscal policy* making Americans go wrong? (11)
  Anagram
14 *Pickled* and *preserved in containers* (6)
  Double definition

16 Said completely to understand *Pope's position* (4,3)
  Additive including **homophone**
19 Cunning method to make *an entrance, perhaps* (7)
  Additive
20 *Rocket* can make one scared, first going off (6)
  Takeaway
22 *He collects a lot*, though record is held by worker (11)
  Sandwich
25 Old Man River is a *standard* (3)
  Additive including **abbreviation**
26 *Give up beef* (5)
  Double definition
27 Wrong choice by opener in *sport* (3,6)
  Additive including **anagram**
28 *Left* section in legal document (8)
  Sandwich
29 *Operator of late ferry* running daily, initially (6)
  Additive

Down

1 *Money* some in Europe set aside (6)
  Hidden
2 Almost risk carrying horse in *vehicle* (9)
  Sandwich including **takeaway**
3 *Brilliance*, and what produces it, say (5)
  Homophone
5 *Group of artists* in rebuilt atelier, perhaps (3-11)
  Anagram

6 Follow and arrest *part of religious outfit* (3,6)
  Additive
7 *People* found as I'm heading North, having crossed South Africa? (5)
  Sandwich including **reversal** and **abbreviation**
8 *Monastic life* is embraced by dimwit with hesitation (8)
  Sandwich

The solution is on page 197

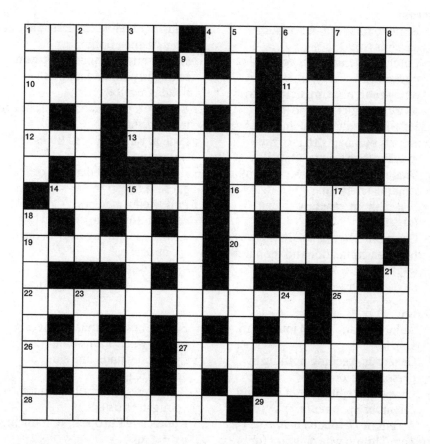

9 *Getting higher in class?* That could make one oddly proud – and will, maybe (8,6)
Anagram

15 Recent delivery of *humorous magazine* (3,6)
Additive

17 In *game of cards*, one who punches the boss? (4,5)
Novelty

18 Cavalryman's equipment kept in rotten *stable* (8)
Sandwich

21 Carbon material, as *alternative to charcoal* (6)
Additive including **abbreviation**

23 *Surpass – blast!* (5)
Double definition

24 *Old-fashioned loyalty* of Communist husband (5)
Additive including **abbreviation**

Practice Puzzle 2:

Across

1. Brute roams wild in botanical gardens (10)
6. Complain vehicle has very little power (4)
9. Shiny coat, note, mislaid when touring part of Europe (5,5)
10. Half-heartedly catch single fish (4)
12. British PC having to face the music – that's novel (8,4)
15. Went off, crossing river west of American city (9)
17. Loiter about, wasting time in bay (5)
18. Court official, one mediating between councillor and monarch (5)

19. Information I've circulated to one woman and another (9)
20. France-gites: new organisation raking in pounds for such a holiday? (4-8)
24. Beastly noise emanating from zoo in Kenya (4)
25. I will say a number of times: 27? (10)
26. Home established at end of garden? (4)
27. Poorly educated and characterless? (10)

Down

1. Sailor heading off on journey in ship (4)
2. Generous, keeping nothing in personal account (4)
3. Lowest possible cost of jam and cereal for Spooner (7,5)
4. Accent in *The Sound of Music*? (5)
5. Tom Thumb was a fighter (9)
7. Was sorry a game plan ultimately proved deficient, when drawn up (10)
8. Old man's ailing more having swallowed liquid form of medicine (10)

11. First of novices that is entering in nunnery is troublesome (12)
13. Eventually finds line's out of action (6,4)
14. Removes skin around fish for youngsters (10)
16. Appreciate European renouncing a drug (9)
21. Lift beams, say (5)
22. Where you'll hear loud song? (4)
23. Absolutely dull (4)

The solution is on pages 198-199

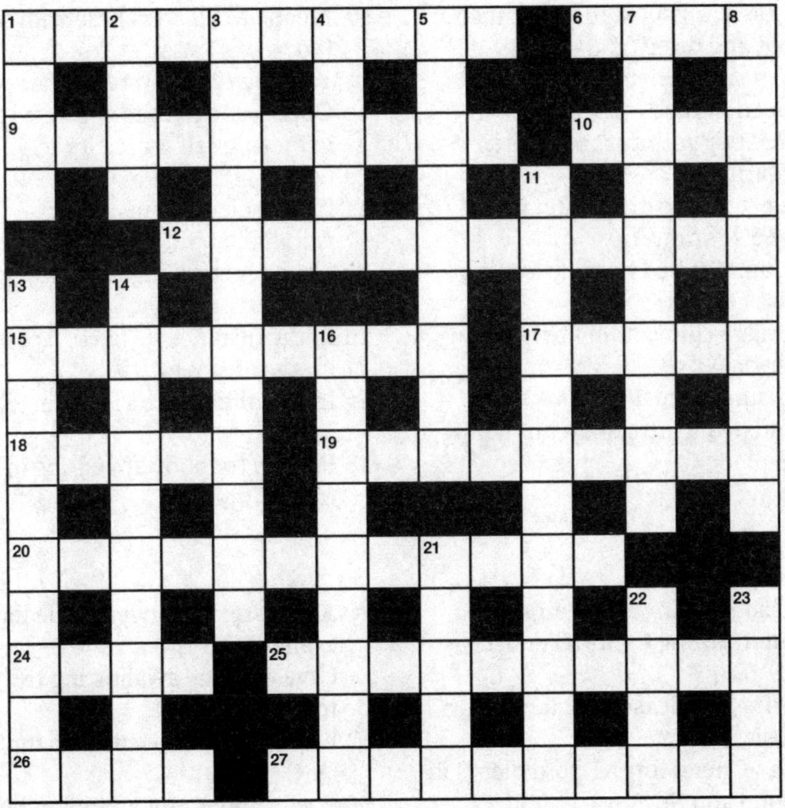

Practice Puzzle 3:

Across

1 Crash impact something that's cut and dried (3,3,3)
6 Warning when about to miss bend in road (5)
9 Be busy with part of kitchen routine (7)
10 Doctor repeating notes about one's tummy (7)
11 Hammer had no time for this director (5)
12 Bridge club coming first getting medal (4,5)
14 Claim interest (3)
15 Inflated hydrogen in hut failing to explode (11)
17 Means to fill crew here with alarm (11)
19 Yob one encountered in fair (3)
20 Opposition parties accordingly gathering call for leader to go (4,3,2)
22 Exercise noisily in ancient woodland (5)
24 Stranger stopping helps foreign girl (7)
26 In the distance lie back, lapping up the cream (7)
27 Irish politician that I got involved in firm (5)
28 Reason for body appearing in fracas? (5,4)

Down

1 That's boring old Henry interrupting Cardinal endlessly (2-3)
2 Miss broadcast after mounting delay (4,3)
3 Base metal forged from pieces in Soho and SE25 (9)
4 Lass giving off smell, one hanging in the air (11)
5 Lift part of spring vegetable plant (3)
6 Like detectives turning up old detection method (5)
7 Rescue from trouble in flight (4,3)
8 Dissident caught escaping from jail after scrap (9)
13 A spinster no longer immediately available (3-3-5)
14 Caves in time swallowing trunk road in city (3,6)
16 Innocent one they will corrupt (4-5)
18 Poet's green: not a lord but boy (7)
19 Nothing wrong with one having a hard book (7)
21 Odd characters from MASH met and taken away in van (5)
23 Resign from French-American college (5)
25 Man not born of woman (3)

The solution is on pages 199-201

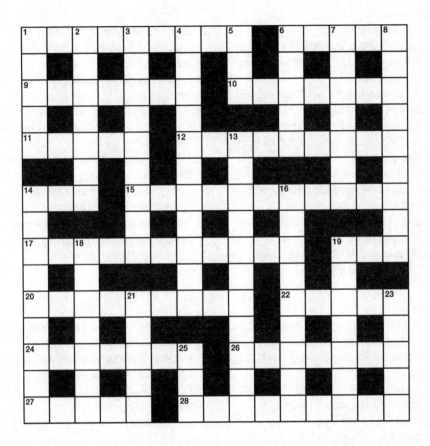

Practice Puzzle 4:

Across

1 Act outrageously, putting a minute hole in trophy (4,2,2)
9 Lacking energy, a race with axes gets you fit (8)
10 Ideal conditions, with plump old woman hugging one! (6)
11 Covering duck a weakness with some cricket commentaries (5-5)
12 Pronounced fit, he was done in before anyone else (4)
13 Hard to admire kid getting old (4,5-1)
16 Event broadcast live in the New Year? (7)
17 Where you'll find something burning in range? (7)
20 Intense campaign settled audience's worries reflected in petition (10)
22 One in exaltation left couples venue (4)
23 Weaving till Lent keeps the French or Spanish orphan in work (6,4)
25 With it, legal document is beyond doubt (6)
26 Succeeded in moving cables following shower of pitch (4,4)
27 Round Britain spikes discovered hidden in pea soup? (8)

Down

2 A postgrad conceals lie spoken by one in biology class (8)
3 Rests under haystack, in part with most needles? (10)
4 A stickler for recycling bottles very green on transport (6-4)
5 Dreadfully anxious to include a name in particular (7)
6 Came to two Kensington houses (4)
7 Happened to live with doctor I didn't like (6)
8 Be prepared for a possible house call! (4,4)
14 Twin brothers hiding leading couple's expensive jewellery (5-5)
15 Little room to embrace radical reform in regional service (5,5)
16 People hope to be placed on their membership lists (3,5)
18 Pole, perhaps, Scotsman stuffed with cord (8)
19 Compromise on deferred issue (4,3)
21 Question in it is in Latin? (2,4)
24 Girl, thoroughly English, from the South (4)

The solution is on pages 201-202

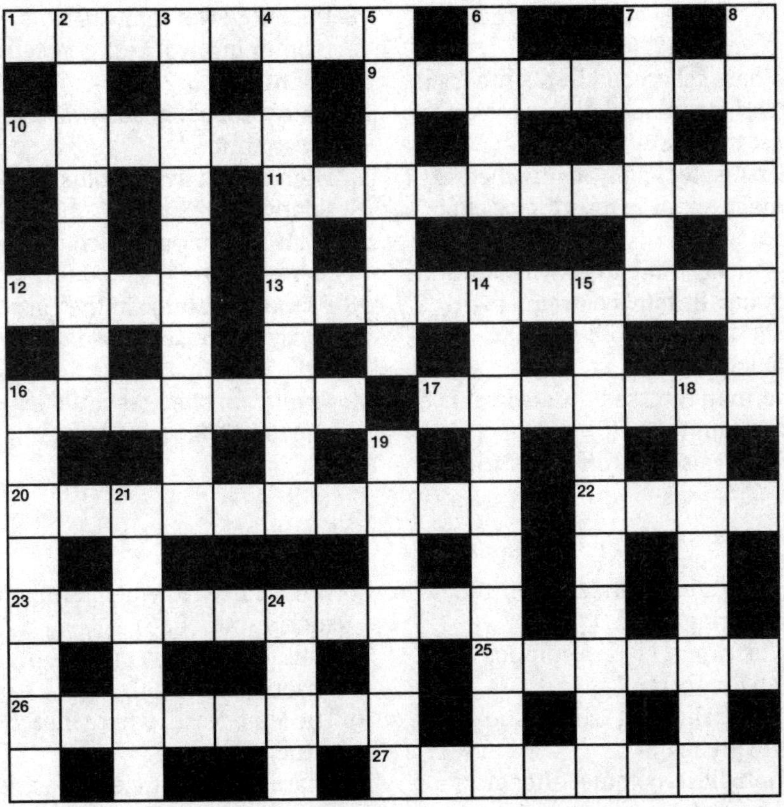

Practice Puzzle 5:

Across

1 Great bloke on pole, the main controller (8)
6 Where schoolchildren snitch? (6)
9 Workers in need of answer get the last word (4)
10 Strange feeling a bit attached to one, beginning to eulogise shoe! (10)
11 A prickly thing to go without God among Britain's extremists (10)
13 Test a number of groups in biology (4)
14 German reversed round a vehicle, it's plain to see (8)
16 Emphasise why off work? (6)
18 Poor dog! Not many get restraining order (6)
20 Might etrol be? (4-4)
22 Dairy product needs wife to call for attention (4)
24 High cost of living holds single relative back (10)
26 Wine has colour which is superior to body (10)
28 Prime minister is in the garden (4)
29 Fancy fish to sell down the river (6)
30 Cryptic finished, as you'd expect one to be? (8)

Down

2 I'm an adult wandering in state bordering Kerala (5,4)
3 Wok expert given a comprehensive fix (7)
4 Open delivering Carnoustie's fifth green (5)
5 Football stand quiet after start of game (3)
6 One's in the subcontinent – north-west of here? (9)
7 Hot food, so blow (7)
8 King, having captured US city, put feet up (5)
12 Play: it starts 'In the beginning', by word of introduction (7)
15 What's needed when jumper in such a state? (3,6)
17 Southern bird over promontory - serious nature! (9)
19 The High Road, where insect settled (7)
21 Charlie seeks articles in fashion (7)
23 Might one be up on this drug? (5)
25 Note always turning up - rare one? (5)
27 Is his brain left redundant? (3)

The solution is on pages 202-204

Practice Puzzle 6:

Across

1 Fast vehicle ahead is a hardtop (8)
5 Assorted pieces (6)
9 Son having Indian food gets runs (8)
10 Prevents further development of hair-raising exploits (6)
12 Writer is available in a foreign edition, pirated (12)
15 Entertainment of old a theatre company rejected (5)
16 Sudden descent downhill makes skier tremble with cold (9)
18 Mostly prevent men going round old part of theatre (5,4)
19 Type of mushroom used in casserole? No kidding (5)
20 French composer almost worth considering (12)
24 Finally decide between right and wrong answer (6)
25 A holm oak's rotten state (8)
26 Issue about getting sister accommodated in pleasant property (3,3)
27 Student, proud to secure a first in divinity at university (8)

Down

1 Performers in stage musical, giving a twirl at the end (4)
2 Bitter herb said to make sauce base (4)
3 Ancestors are not recorded in part of book (9)
4 A-level body must support oral examiner: it's laid out in black and white (12)
6 Old man's half-hearted talk (5)
7 Working on mini-cars for stars (5,5)
8 Be careful of morally suspect female's charm (4,4,2)
11 Drama teacher's unusual interpretation meets resistance (3,9)
13 Thought about assigning right and left wingers to team (10)
14 Woman's account inflamed American philosopher (10)
17 Employee on board keeps sailors near rear of ship (9)
21 Lighter piece of metal, say, can be lifted (5)
22 US state initiating investigation of Watergate aftermath (4)
23 Given accommodation in flat, I settled (4)

The solution is on pages 204-205

Practice Puzzle 7:

Across
1 Mates heading off to fantastic part of France (6)
4 A boy tucked into grain, having added salt (8)
10 Bird or rock rabbit? (9)
11 Sign off, say, when retiring (5)
12 Slight suspicion fish ejected liquid (3)
13 Has second thoughts about conditions in which English politicians are kept (11)
14 I eat spinach and fish you served (6)
16 Female rider falls during dressage, losing heart (7)
19 One part of the Bible: part of the Old Testament, actually (2,5)
20 To members of audience, players sounded fed up (6)
22 Unable to manoeuvre forty gallons or so? (4,1,6)
25 Male loves unpopular woman (3)
26 After start of offensive, soldiers leave distant region (5)
27 Discussion of NHS care? (9)
28 Reserve little time for visiting holiday resort (3,5)
29 Language suppressed by anger management (6)

Down
1 Engineer using gold – singular kind of metal (6)
2 Place to store wine (9)
3 Food and drink down in price – dropping a penny (5)
5 Daughter restricted by rare digestion trouble ... having this? (6,8)
6 Minor railway track sinking into the ground (9)
7 Jog with no clothes on and you'll get good hiding (5)
8 Island's judge put off accepting European finance system (8)
9 Yellow and red suit briefly worn by fashionable fellows (7-7)
15 Trainers sorted out our cadets (9)
17 Fancy a drink with meal to begin with? The perfect combination (5,4)
18 Tailless mousy trio scurries about showing fear (8)
21 Dumpling puts weight on – a lot of weight! (6)
23 Demand divorcee put before a court (5)
24 Piece of wood placed on end of the artisan's machine (5)

Practice Puzzle 8:

Across

1 A revolutionary plan going round the educational community (8)
6 So-called person beating the booze (6)
9 Characters involved in Shakespearean plot (4)
10 What pyromaniac must do furiously (4,6)
11 Very, very good standard not welcomed in the main (5,5)
13 Give spanking good smack (4)
14 Pain and misfortune – yet one remains optimistic (8)
16 Offensive radio broadcast about noon (6)
18 Dash outside with criminal (6)
20 What may be drunk by a politician is dependent on chance (8)
22 Successfully secures a great deal (4)
24 Craft needed by person with failing party? (3-7)
26 Ecstasy obtained from him servant adulterated (10)
28 Romantic couple's bit of news (4)
29 Crowning moment of the second of *Three Men In A Boat* (6)
30 Ruin song with one dance move that's not quiet (3,5)

Down

2 Diamonds are real, asked initially? Sauce! (9)
3 Suffering from a number of blows (4,3)
4 Cheeky madam finally moves to the front in panic (5)
5 Article written on British diver (3)
6 His policy: carrying one to bed when husband's away? (9)
7 Somewhere to live down south for three months (7)
8 Duck is able to cross Eastern Pacific (5)
12 See red after game's over (2,5)
15 Tell me quickly what's unfashionable and fashionable! (3,4,2)
17 A welcome home for chaps in union (9)
19 Striking as blade might be (7)
21 A Catherine that had Sinatra smitten? (7)
23 Saying of Lovelace, say, has turned up (5)
25 Upsetting salt over turkey wings could make one cross (5)
27 Fish given in list (after horse) (3)

The solution is on pages 207-208

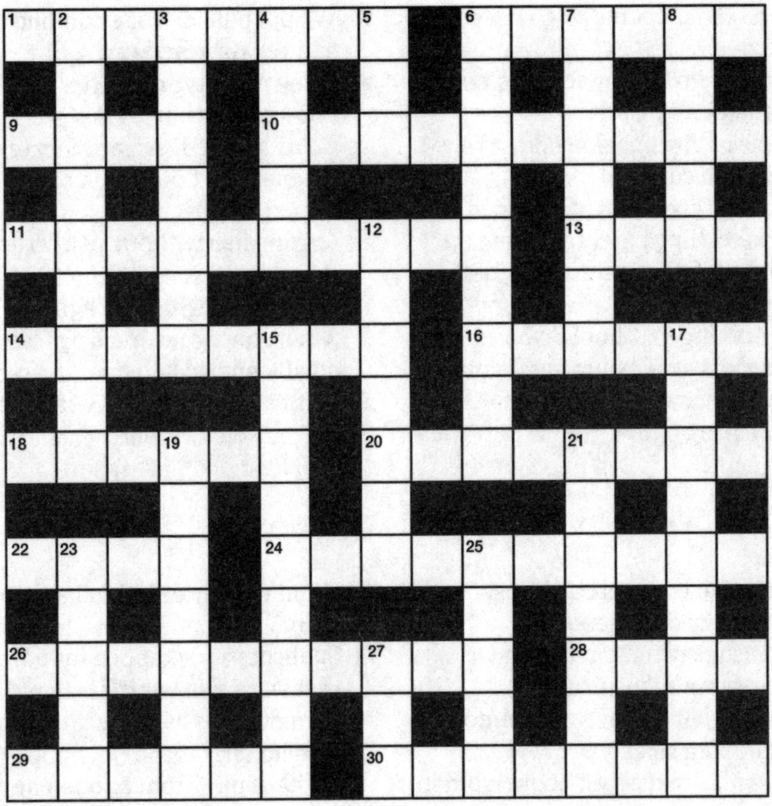

Practice Puzzle 9:

Across
1 First fop prepared to go naked? (5,3)
5 Advise what Pam needs to take pain (6)
9 Way of bowling done deviously through cover (9)
11 Send to specialist, concerned with iron reading barely showing (5)
12 Church father's returning hot treasure (7)
13 Confining to school involves Rugby's head being harsh (7)
14 Prestige owner arranged for help in driving (5,8)

16 We pot blue – shot's complicated and very involved (2,2,3,6)
20 What will have character shortly immersed in here? (7)
21 Good-natured? A fine story (7)
23 Cleaner's put marks on small ornament (5)
24 Cutting fish without right article takes time (9)
25 Ultimately right to be agitated when son's gone missing – as a small child will do (6)
26 With complete year's guarantee (8)

Down
1 Artificial channel cut across middle of obstruction (6)
2 British leaving to make way across watershed... (5)
3 ...experience range with almost unlimited vista (7)
4 What's great about obese woman chasing achievement as a boxer (13)
6 Tell managed to get up speed (7)
7 Where boundaries must have been crossed if film's to get broadcast (3-6)
8 Tons keep quiet when entering into extra borrowing arrangement (8)

10 What's made only to snap in bits? (7,6)
14 Sponsorship scrapped for pageant that lacks following (9)
15 Tom perhaps asked what's new in camera (8)
17 Perhaps play from another suit over hearts, securing one win (7)
18 Policeman in charge in bid for acceptance (7)
19 Somewhere in church match shortly is concluded with lines (6)
22 This is strong meat (5)

The solution is on pages 208-209

Practice Puzzle 10:

Across

1 Stonework produced by girl carrying child (7)
5 African – his room needs refurbishment (7)
9 Put up with limit after I left for university (9)
10 Tool causing a sudden problem (5)
11 American serviceman sent back to smallest room in White House (5)
12 Gordon led astray, making a bloomer (9)
13 Some drivers do remain inconspicuous (4,1,4,4)
17 Dispatched to island, people correspond in mawkish fashion (13)
21 Vamp is about to reform? On the contrary (9)
24 Block off nearby cul-de-sac (5)
25 Endow part of a hospital (5)
26 Love car with top removed for holding party in the open air (3-2-4)
27 Showing impatience, say, going back inside too soon (7)
28 Historian city's heard of (7)

Down

1 Do one's share, putting up with family (6)
2 Give information and reveal just one thing (9)
3 To develop business contacts, new serviceman has introduced a couple (7)
4 Racy rogue's prepared address (4,5)
5 Copper possibly had an encounter with gangster (5)
6 Out of condition, almost sickly-looking – but not in the rush hour (3-4)
7 Meet with popular scoundrel (5)
8 They ride out to get what's coming to them (8)
14 Genuine article accepted by family member in charge (9)
15 Confused? Go to Ely, my original source (9)
16 Stop making reptile cross (8)
18 Monks are suitable (2,5)
19 A match for Venus (7)
20 Step, jade green, worn away at edges (6)
22 Paramedics initially called to crash (5)
23 Elemental sarcasm (5)

The solution is on pages 209-210

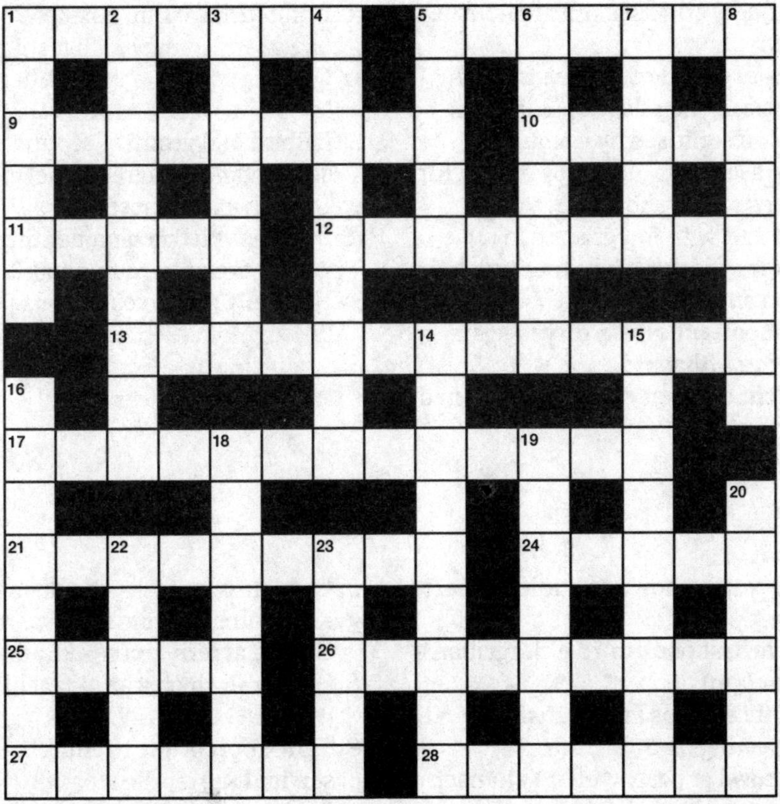

Practice Puzzle 11:

Across

1 Loudly criticises private housing (8)
9 Brief sound of glasses touching twice, when this is said? (4-4)
10 Man confused by events (6)
11 Was initially unhappy to do a turn in farewell show (10)
12 Barrel with top grade fish (4)
13 It may result in another hearing, on appeal (10)
16 Important match played again after setback (7)
17 Soldier or cadet has to be trained (7)
20 Done with wealth, possibly? (4,2,4)
22 Oddly ignored sexy Greek heroine (4)
23 Jailbird and group of scoundrels showing no disagreement (10)
25 Upset, wearing green (6)
26 One about to keep on fighting getting weighty equipment (8)
27 Naturally preserves various items (8)

Down

2 Pictures shown to audience here (3,5)
3 The last book to give clergyman joy? (10)
4 Officer steps in to transform meeting (10)
5 Crowd at party with no stomach for rough drink (7)
6 Coal supplier makes a bomb (4)
7 After cold starter, I provided hot dish (6)
8 Prisoner's short time to find where PC gets information (8)
14 Go to inhale crack – it's divine (10)
15 Kept going, getting travel permit clipped at ferry port (6,4)
16 Had a role in charge of teaching (8)
18 Tune appropriate to church service (3,5)
19 Say what inventor does for town (7)
21 Unrestrained soldier conquered all around (6)
24 Certainly no counterfeit coin (4)

The solution is on pages 211-212

Practice Puzzle 12:

Across

1 Bloom lady-killer put back in buttonhole (10)
6 Pot for reheated meat and vegetables (4)
8 Like young female swimmer saved by male (8)
9 When speaking, made fun of a group leader (6)
10 Old soldiers retreating? Captain brought to book (4)
11 Unexpected pair implicated in US-backed insurgency (10)
12 Teacher's instruction after question's answered without effort (5,4)
14 Shows effect of strain in fights (5)
17 Dog brought back hares about end of hunt (5)
19 Not quite enough to make up two teams for a game (6-3)
22 Fascinating woman jailed after tussle about love and deception (5,5)
23 German banker circulating two notes (4)
24 Most appealing version of film is French (6)
25 Undeveloped island on which explorer briefly lands (8)
26 Unconscious immediately after start of boxing match (4)
27 Having moral principles, objected to drunk being given precedence (4,6)

Down

1 American people given care of seventy percent of city (9)
2 They've made tracks and left wearing shortened garments (7)
3 Lad dines out in part of airport (8)
4 Chant questioning restaurant staff's raison d'être? (3,3,2,7)
5 Look for respect (6)
6 Top setter supplying solution (9)
7 Longing to have animals raised in part of the capital (7)
13 Easing of hostilities ends prematurely around border, resulting in damage (9)
15 In various parades ambassador's taken lead (9)
16 Means of transmitting messages installed in teleprinter commonly (8)
18 Academic at university has little time for penitent politician (7)
20 Gothic script expert? (3,4)
21 Find fault with endless razzmatazz at church (6)

The solution is on pages 212-213

17: Leaving the Best Till Last

'Snooker devotee Grace Culmer has given up the game at the age of 101 because she can no longer tell the coloured balls apart. She has told friends she will do crosswords instead.' The Independent

If you have got this far, you deserve a treat, so here is one puzzle which should provide special enjoyment. It has been hailed as one of the best ever to have been published in *The Times*; it is also rather hard, taking seasoned *Times* competitors longer than usual.

I have prepared the clues in three formats so you can try the format that you think is most appropriate to your skill level:

1. As it appeared in *The Times*.
2. Definitions *italicized*;
3. Definitions *italicized*, indicators <u>underlined</u>.

Full solution notes are also provided and they could repay detailed study.

1. Puzzle exactly as it appeared in *The Times*

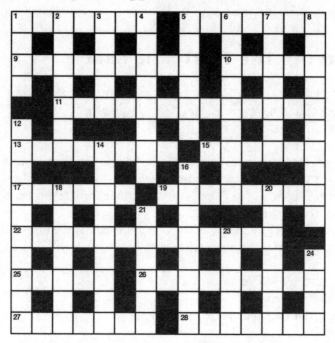

Across

1 Left a van outside? Look out for him! (7)
5 Jerusalem singers pop back for a sneaky listen (7)
9 Male rock DJ guides were wrong about (9)
10 Malicious type more like a celebrity (5)
11 Style of architecture as seen in some clinics, sadly (13)
13 A clergyman, stutteringly faithful (8)
15 Beer bottles on hold (6)
17 Having no good accommodation could shock (6)
19 One state has turned into another (8)
22 Medical institution with back-to-front priorities? (5,8)
25 Country admitted charity is of eastern origin (5)
26 Great Britain's derelict houses all but devoid of capital (9)
27 Incoherent follower of fashion? (7)
28 Eats bananas bound for café (7)

See solution on pages 181–183

Down

1 Not Italy's biggest lake, but equal second? (4)
2 Barrister regularly goes to prison, being brief for killer (7)
3 Remote orbiter's power line knocked out (5)
4 Weapon raised, took control (8)
5 Wicket that is most unplayable for batsman? (6)
6 Girl turned in guns, soldiers alarmed by them? (9)
7 Run outside surgery before surgeon's first cut (7)
8 Soldier right to leave Marines, suffering mental illness (10)
12 Giving smart kit that's also provided in final (10)
14 Author nicked over forged dollar covers (5,4)
16 Road race (or should that be 'road rage'?) (8)
18 Thin girl's bottom shown in poster (7)
20 Not caught, Sam perhaps remains free (7)
21 Outlaw's first offence recorded but it doesn't have to be initialled (6)
23 An OK place like Luton doesn't need working over (5)
24 Move waste paper bags (4)

2. Puzzle with definitions italicized

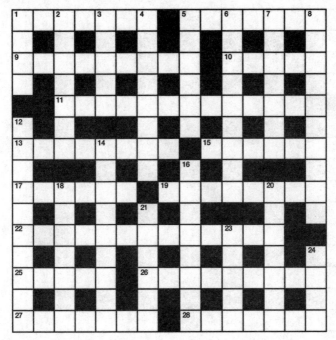

Across

1 Left a van outside? *Look out for him!* (7)
5 Jerusalem singers pop back *for a sneaky listen* (7)
9 Male rock DJ guides *were wrong about* (9)
10 *Malicious type* more like a celebrity (5)
11 *Style of architecture* as seen in some clinics, sadly (13)
13 A clergyman, stutteringly *faithful* (8)
15 Beer bottles on *hold* (6)
17 Having no good accommodation could *shock* (6)
19 One state has turned into *another* (8)
22 *Medical institution with back-to-front priorities?* (5,8)
25 *Country* admitted charity is of eastern origin (5)
26 *Great* Britain's derelict houses all but devoid of capital (9)
27 *Incoherent* follower of fashion? (7)
28 Eats bananas bound for *café* (7)

See solution on pages 181-183

Down

1 *Not Italy's biggest lake*, but equal second? (4)
2 Barrister regularly goes to prison, being brief for *killer* (7)
3 *Remote orbiter's* power line knocked out (5)
4 Weapon raised, took *control* (8)
5 Wicket that is *most unplayable for batsman?* (6)
6 Girl turned in guns, *soldiers alarmed by them?* (9)
7 Run outside surgery before surgeon's first *cut* (7)
8 Soldier right to leave Marines, suffering *mental illness* (10)
12 *Giving smart kit* that's also provided in final (10)
14 *Author* nicked over forged dollar covers (5,4)
16 Road race (*or should that be 'road rage'?*) (8)
18 *Thin* girl's bottom shown in poster (7)
20 Not caught, Sam perhaps remains *free* (7)
21 *Outlaw's* first offence recorded but it doesn't have to be initialled (6)
23 *An OK place* like Luton doesn't need working over (5)
24 *Move* waste paper bags (4)

3. Puzzle with definitions italicized, indicators underlined

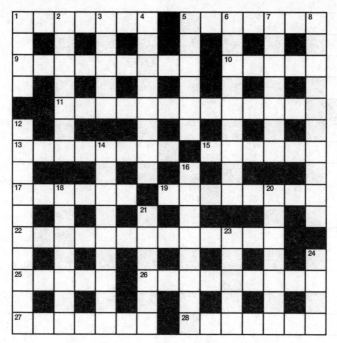

Across

1 Left a van <u>outside</u>? *Look out for him!* (7)
5 Jerusalem singers pop <u>back</u> *for a sneaky listen* (7)
9 Male <u>rock</u> DJ guides *were wrong about* (9)
10 *Malicious type* more like a celebrity (5)
11 *Style of architecture* as seen in some clinics, <u>sadly</u> (13)
13 A clergyman, stutteringly *faithful* (8)
15 Beer <u>bottles</u> on *hold* (6)
17 Having <u>no</u> good accommodation could *shock* (6)
19 One state has <u>turned into</u> *another* (8)
22 *Medical institution* with back-to-front priorities? (5,8)
25 *Country* admitted charity is of <u>eastern origin</u> (5)
26 *Great* Britain's <u>derelict houses</u> all but devoid of capital (9)
27 *Incoherent* follower of fashion? (7)
28 Eats <u>bananas</u> bound for *café* (7)

See solution on pages 181-183

Down

1 *Not Italy's biggest lake*, but equal second? (4)
2 Barrister regularly goes to prison, <u>being brief</u> for *killer* (7)
3 *Remote orbiter*'s power line <u>knocked</u> out (5)
4 Weapon <u>raised</u>, took *control* (8)
5 Wicket that is *most unplayable for batsman?* (6)
6 Girl <u>turned in</u> guns, *soldiers alarmed by them?* (9)
7 Run <u>outside</u> surgery before surgeon's first *cut* (7)
8 Soldier right <u>to leave</u> Marines, <u>suffering</u> *mental illness* (10)
12 *Giving smart kit* that's also provided <u>in</u> final (10)
14 *Author* <u>nicked over</u> forged dollar <u>covers</u> (5,4)
16 Road race (*or should that be 'road rage'?*) (8)
18 *Thin* girl's bottom <u>shown in</u> poster (7)
20 <u>Not</u> caught, Sam perhaps remains *free* (7)
21 *Outlaw's* first offence recorded but it doesn't have to be initialled (6)
23 *An OK place* like Luton <u>doesn't need</u> working <u>over</u> (5)
24 *Move* waste paper <u>bags</u> (4)

Here is the annotated solution:

<table>
<tr><td>C</td><td>L</td><td>A</td><td>M</td><td>P</td><td>E</td><td>R</td><td></td><td>W</td><td>I</td><td>R</td><td>E</td><td>T</td><td>A</td><td>P</td></tr>
</table>

Across		
1	Left a van outside? Look out for him! **Sandwich** including **abbreviation**	**CLAMPER** l in camper
5	Jerusalem singers pop back for a sneaky listen **Additive** including **reversal** and **abbreviation**	**WIRETAP** WI + pater rev
9	Male rock DJ guides were wrong about **Additive** including **anagram**	**MISJUDGED** m + (DJ guides)*
10	Malicious type more like a celebrity **Novelty**	**VIPER** VIPer (invented comparative)

11 Style of architecture as seen in some clinics, sadly **Anagram** including **sandwich**	**NEOCLASSICISM** as in (some clinics)*
13 A clergyman, stutteringly faithful **Novelty**	**ACCURATE** a c-curate
15 Beer bottles on hold **Sandwich**	**ALLEGE** leg = on in ale
17 Having no good accommodation could shock **Additive** including **take away**	**DISMAY** digs minus g + may
19 One state has turned into another **Sandwich** including **abbreviation**	**MISSOURI** is sour reversed in MI (not reversed)
22 Medical institution with back-to-front priorities? **Cryptic definition**	**FIELD HOSPITAL** back to the front (line)
25 Country admitted charity is of eastern origin **Additive** including **reversal**	**INDIA** in = admitted + aid reversed
26 Great Britain's derelict houses all but devoid of capital **Sandwich** including **anagram**	**BRILLIANT** (a)ll in Britain*
27 Incoherent follower of fashion? **Novelty**	**GARBLED** garb-led
28 Eats bananas bound for café **Additive** including **anagram**	**TEASHOP** eats* + hop

Down

1 Not Italy's biggest lake, but equal second? **Additive**	**COMO** co-mo

2	Barrister regularly goes to prison, being brief for killer **Additive** including two **take aways**	**ARSENIC** (b)a(r)r(i)s(t)e(r) + nic(k)
3	Remote orbiter's power line knocked out **Additive** including **anagram**	**PLUTO** P + l = line + out*
4	Weapon raised, took control **Additive** including **reversal**	**REGULATE:** luger reversed + ate
5	Wicket that is most unplayable for batsman? **Additive**	**WIDEST** w + id est
6	Girl turned in guns, soldiers alarmed by them? **Sandwich** including **reversal**	**REVEILLES:** Ellie reversed in revs
7	Run outside surgery before surgeon's first cut **Sandwich** including **abbreviation**	**TOPSIDE:** op + s(urgeon) in tide
8	Soldier right to leave Marines, suffering mental illness **Additive** including **anagram** and **takeaway**	**PARAMNESIA** para + ma(r)ines*
12	Giving smart kit that's also provided in final **Sandwich**	**DANDIFYING** and + if in dying
14	Author nicked over forged dollar covers **Sandwich** including **reversal** and **anagram**	**ROALD DAHL** had reversed in dollar*
16	Road race (or should that be 'road rage'?) **Additive**	**MISPRINT** MI + sprint
18	Thin girl's bottom shown in poster **Sandwich** including **take away**	**SLENDER** l in sender
20	Not caught, Sam perhaps remains free **Additive** including **take away**	**UNLEASH** Un(c)le + ash

21 Outlaw's first offence recorded but it doesn't have to be initialled **Additive**	**FORBID** **initial letters**
23 An OK place like Luton doesn't need working over **Reversal** including **take away**	**TULSA: as + Lut(on)** **all reversed**
24 Move waste paper bags **Hidden**	**STEP** **waste paper**

This particular puzzle received a good reception from those who comment daily on *Times* puzzles, the bloggers (see Chapter 15). Here are some of their comments.

- '... a superbly innovative crossword. In my opinion this is exactly what a modern-day Times puzzle ought to be, and I raise my hat to the setter. The answer to 26 across sums it up: BRILLIANT. In fact having looked at it again I'm not sure that it isn't the best Times cryptic I've ever solved!!! Pretty well every clue is a gem.'

- 'Absolutely brilliant. The first time in years that I've needed more than an hour to finish a puzzle. I reckon 1 hour 20 minutes in all, allowing for breaks. At 23 down I looked at T?L?A for goodness knows how long before I saw OK = Oklahoma. I don't think there's a duff clue among them.

- 'I have to record a solving time of 26 m:43 s ... which means that I found this very tough indeed, especially the SW corner.'

- 'There's no really difficult vocabulary or clues that seem unfair – just lots of very good disguise. A definite win for the setter. I stopped bothering to put 'clever combination of wordplay and surface' as it happens so often. If there's any other contender for puzzle of the week, we're in for some treats.'

18: Evolution of *The Times* Crossword

'Let us grasp the situation. Solve the complicated plot.' WS Gilbert,
The Gondoliers

It should be clear by now that I admire *The Times* Crossword and consider it
has no need to change its successful, long-standing style but in this final
chapter I'm setting out some ideas which could improve the solver
experience.

1. Setter name disclosure

From the beginning, *Times* setters have been unnamed. Increasingly however
over recent years, setters in other newspapers and magazines have been
identified by either pseudonyms or real names. These include the
Independent, the *Financial Times*, the *Guardian* and weekly media such as
The Sunday Times, the *Sunday Telegraph*, the *Observer*, *The Week*, the *Oldie*
and the *Spectator*. Even the *Daily Telegraph* is following this trend four days a
week with its Toughie puzzle.

There are some arguments in favour of *The Times* adopting this trend:

- It would help solvers become even more familiar with their daily
  'tormentors'. Regular solvers would enjoy spotting the individual
  characteristics and style of a named setter.
- It would help to keep setters on their toes. Good though the editor
  undoubtedly is at maintaining high standards, a little extra internal
  competition would do no harm and may even help to raise standards
  further.
- Most of the original material in the newspaper is attributed so why not
  the crossword, especially in view of its significance to the readership?
- It would give setters the recognition they deserve.

The Times held out longest of all newspapers with advertisements rather than
news on its front page, maybe it will be the last to publicise its setters.

2. Living people

Crosswords appearing in most if not all the puzzles mentioned above sometimes include living people as solutions or as part of the wordplay. This results in some topical and fun clues and it would be good to see *The Times* restriction lifted. One of *The Times* Saturday puzzles (the *Listener* crossword) evidently is not so constrained so that superb clues like this appear therein:

ADDITIVE CLUE: Where you focus on Turner, for example (6)

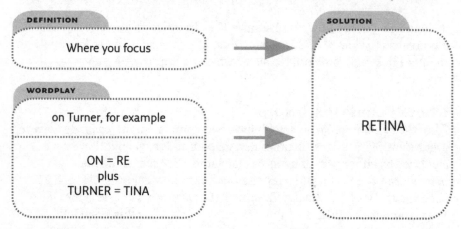

DEFINITION		SOLUTION
Where you focus	→	
WORDPLAY		RETINA
on Turner, for example	→	
ON = RE plus TURNER = TINA		

3. Themed puzzles

A relatively recent development within daily puzzles is the inclusion of themes. As an example, the *Independent* at the time of the 2007 rugby world cup published a puzzle by Virgilius, including a grid with rugby posts and rugby-related clues. Whilst not everyone may welcome this sort of thing, my surveys of workshop participants show that themes are much enjoyed. As far as I know, the only such puzzles published by *The Times* have been one for John Betjeman's centenary and another in May 2008 to coincide with the launch of *Devil May Care*. This one was well received by bloggers, attracting more comment than usual on the daily puzzle. 'What a pity there are not more (themed puzzles),' wrote one, echoing my sentiments.

PART 4

APPENDICES

Appendices

'I'm going to do a crossword with Miss Abbott. Mr Merryman is Ximenes standard.'
'I'm a Times *man myself,' Alleyn said.*

Ngaio Marsh, *Singing in the Shrouds*

1. Abbreviations

The list that follows is by no means 'official'. It is one I have built up myself but it does include most of the abbreviations that have appeared in *The Times* Crossword in recent years. To faciliate your solving, they are arranged in order of the abbreviated word rather than the abbreviation.

a	A	caught	C	ecstasy	E
about	A,C, CA, RE	century	C	energy	E
		chapter	C	engineers	RE
abstemious	TT	church	CE, CH	English	E
ace	A	circle	O	female	F
against	V	city	EC, LA, NY	fifty	L
ambassador	HE			fine	F
answer	A	class	CL	five	V
are	A	clubs	C	five hundred	D
area	A	cold	C	following	F
artist	RA	Conservative	C	forte	F
bachelor	B	copper	CU	frequency	F
bishop	B, RR	daughter	D	gallons	G
black	B	departs	D	gold	AU, OR
book	B, VOL	diamonds	D		
books	NT, OT	died	D	good	G
		doctor	DR, MO, MB	graduate	MA, BA, MBA
born	B				
bowled	B				
breadth	B	double round	OO	grand	G
British	B,BR	drug	E,H	gunners	RA
brown	BR	duke	D	gym	PE
bye	B	east(ern)	E	hard	H

has	S	noon	N	silver	AG
hearts	H	north(ern)	N	singular	S
height	H	nothing	O	son	S
henry	H	nought	O	south(ern)	S
heroin	H	of	O	spades	S
horse	H	old	O	stone	ST
hospital	H	one	I or UN	street	ST
hot	H			succeeded	S
hour	H	page	P	Switzerland	CH
hundred	C	painter	RA	tango	T
husband	H	pawn	P	temperature	T
iron	Fe	penny, pence	P	thousand	K, M
is	S	piano	P	time	T
island	I	posh	U	ton(s)	T
Jack	J	potassium	K	town	T
Judge	J	pound	L	union	NUT, NUR
King	K, R, GR	power	P		
		pressure	P	united	U
kiss	X	queen	Q, R, ER, HM	universal	U
knight	N			university	U
knighthood	K	question	Q	upper-class	U
lake	L	quiet	P	versus	V
learner	L	race(s)	TT	velocity	V
left	L	rating	AB	very	V
Liberal	L	record	EP, LP	verse	V
line	L, RY	resistance	R	volume	V
litre	L	right	R	vote, sign of error	
love	O	ring	O		X
maiden	M	river	R	way	AVE, RD, ST
male	M	road	RD		
mark(s)	M	rook	R	weight	W
married	M	run(s)	R	west(ern)	W
masculine	M	sailor	AB	wicket	W
mass	M	saint	S, ST	wide	W
men	M, OR	seaman	AB	width	W
mile	M	second(s)	S	wife	W
million(s)	M	see	V, C	with	W
minute(s)	M	service	RN	women's	W
monarch	ER	shirt	T	yard	Y
Monsieur	M	short time	M, MIN, MO, S, SEC, T	year(s)	Y
motorway	M, MI			yen	Y
name	N			zero	O
new	N				
newton	N				
nitrogen	N				

2. Clues to try – solutions

As before, anagram fodder indicated by an asterisk; indicators <u>underlined</u>.

ANAGRAM CLUES

1   Adhesive tapes <u>come unstuck</u>.
     Tapes*   **PASTE**

2   One could claim <u>damages</u> à la rugby.
     A la rugby*   **ARGUABLY**

3   It's a crime <u>breaking</u> a truce.
     It's a crime*   **ARMISTICE**

4   Need AGM <u>arranged</u> close to board meeting.
     Need AGM*   **ENDGAME**

5   Gee – Old Glory <u>ill befits</u> British PM!
     Gee Old Glory*   **LLOYD GEORGE**

6   Anti-abortionist <u>fixed</u> it for the girl.
     It for the girl*   **RIGHT-TO-LIFER**

7   Tip of offensive hardware <u>being shot</u>.
     O = tip of offensive + **hardware***   **ARROWHEAD**

8   Old man takes violin <u>to play</u> in summerhouse.
     Pa + **violin***   **PAVILION**

9   International meetings – often scenic summer <u>thrashes</u>?
     Often scenic summer*   **SUMMIT CONFERENCES**

10   Break down after <u>moving</u> letters from close pal.
     Close pal*   **COLLAPSE**

SANDWICH CLUES

1   Shock seeing *Times* leader <u>in</u> unlikely location.
     T in **sun**   **STUN**

2   It may make us take shelter <u>in</u> centre of Boston.
     Lee in **St**   **SLEET**

3   Scrap copper <u>collected by</u> motor sport bodies.
     Cu in **F1 stiffs**   **FISTICUFFS**

4   Lacking the will <u>to cross</u> river between parts of US.
     R in **intestate**   **INTERSTATE**

5   Time <u>in</u> cell? But one isn't charged.
     T in **neuron**   **NEUTRON**

6	Left tart after <u>eating</u> slice of apple and cheese. **Port** + **a** in **slut**	**PORT SALUT**
7	Go on bed <u>inside which</u> there's a rat! **Turn** + **a** in **cot**	**TURNCOAT**
8	Incy Wincy Spider, say, caught <u>in</u> rain, had gone up the spout. **C** = caught in **rain had***	**ARACHNID**
9	Hunt the writer <u>in</u> a way that's cunning. **Leigh** in **St**	**SLEIGHT**
10	Indigestion? A most <u>troubled</u> hour <u>in</u> store! **Most*** + **h** in **cache**	**STOMACH ACHE**

TAKE AWAY CLUES

1	It's better <u>avoided by</u> one renouncing alcohol. **Better** minus **TT**	**BEER**
2	Enthusiastic call from people <u>losing</u> head and heart. **Men** minus **m** + **core**	**ENCORE**
3	<u>No</u> time for nurse's work – that's final! **Tending** minus **t**	**ENDING**
4	Old scientist agreed to cut a holiday <u>short</u>. **Chimed** in **a rest** minus **t**	**ARCHIMEDES**
5	Singer in state of nudity? Get her <u>off</u>! **Altogether** minus **get her**	**ALTO**
6	Perhaps unwisely hospital's <u>gone</u> private. **Perhaps*** minus **h**	**SAPPER**
7	<u>First off</u> most harsh mountain. **Severest** minus **S**	**EVEREST**
8	Administrators are <u>at heart</u> grey men. **Grey** minus **G y** + **gents**	**REGENTS**
9	<u>Take tip</u> from champion craftsman. **Partisan** minus **P**	**ARTISAN**
10	Perhaps a lorry needs <u>empty</u> lane. **Artic** + **lane** minus **an**	**ARTICLE**

LETTER SWITCH CLUES

1	Source of inspiration to preach '<u>the first shall be last and...</u>' **O** and **e** swapped in **orate**	**ERATO**

2	What is <u>replacing</u> a tricky contest? **Is** replacing **a** in **what**	**WHIST**
3	Queen of France <u>has replaced</u> one divine female. **I** in **reine** moved	**IRENE**
4	Do a <u>heart transplant</u> for Tom. **C** in **he-cat** moved	**CHEAT**
5	Fish <u>moves</u> south along the coast. **S** = south in **seashore** moves to the right	**SEA HORSE**
6	Resigned after editor's <u>move</u> to change structure. Move **ed** within **resigned**	**REDESIGN**
7	<u>Change of direction</u> at end of dangerous river. **N** = north for **e** = east in **severe**	**SEVERN**
8	Struggled getting roast <u>out of one oven into another</u>. **Roast** minus **oast** in **stove**	**STROVE**

REVERSAL CLUES

1	At short notice, <u>send back</u> information. **At** + **ad** reversed	**DATA**
2	Indian governor <u>sent back</u> in run out. **He** reversed in **run***	**NEHRU**
3	<u>After retirement</u>, go round the bend. **Stab** reversed	**BATS**
4	Save from boat <u>capsizing</u> [down clue]. **But** = **save from** reversed	**TUB**
5	Given money back <u>on return</u> of this napkin. **Repaid** reversed	**DIAPER**
6	Fabric that's the <u>reverse of</u> a bargain – rubbish! **Snip** reversed + **tripe**	**PINSTRIPE**
7	Revealing material writer <u>turned up</u> [down clue]. **Eliot** reversed	**TOILE**
8	Ties <u>up</u> this turf [down clue]. **Draws** reversed	**SWARD**
9	Did some work at last, <u>having turned up</u> in Greek Island [down clue]. **Soled** reversed	**DELOS**

10	Huge flans <u>all round</u> – that's the trick! **Mega tarts** reversed	STRATAGEM

HIDDEN CLUES

1	Swimmer <u>turning in</u> special pool.	PLAICE
2	Slight item <u>coming between</u> raisin and sultana.	INSULT
3	Mount Vesuvius strikes, engulfing Naples, <u>taking just seconds</u>.	ETNA
4	<u>Some</u> unceremonious language.	SLANG
5	Novel <u>penned by</u> Alessandro Manzoni.	ROMAN
6	Roof space full of these <u>boxes</u>.	LOFT
7	Sensation <u>concealed by</u> Chopin, Sand needlessly.	PINS AND NEEDLES
8	Some job at hand? We'll soon <u>see</u>.	BATH AND WELLS (a see)
9	She's repeatedly <u>kept in</u> bed – it helped, I think.	EDITH
10	<u>Happy</u> perhaps being involved in battlefield warfare.	DWARF

HOMOPHONE CLUES

1	<u>Part</u> of the church where one hears 'I will'.	AISLE
2	Man's <u>spoken of</u> busy junction.	CREWE
3	<u>Sound</u> battery to dispose of.	SELL
4	Taken in school – <u>oral</u>.	EATEN
5	Composer close to Britten <u>in sound</u>.	IRELAND
6	Planet revolved rapidly, <u>we hear</u>.	WORLD (whirled)
7	Courtiers <u>heard</u> building fences.	PALISADES
8	Green space to disappear, <u>it's said</u> – stop using the car!	HYDE PARK
9	Superior sort of busybody, <u>say</u>.	PRIOR
10	Weapon in front of ship? <u>Doesn't sound like it</u>.	BOW

ALL-IN-ONE CLUES

1	Who carried the can, losing head <u>sadly</u>? **Who carried the can*** minus **C**	CATHERINE HOWARD
2	<u>What could be</u> the last course? That's about right. **R** + **the last course***	CHARLOTTE RUSSE

3	A nit is often the <u>product of this</u>. **A nit is often***	**INFESTATION**
4	Real patriots <u>after revolution</u>? **Real patriots***	**PROLETARIATS**
5	Time we have <u>to hold</u> start of lunch. **T + l** in **we've**	**TWELVE**
6	Reverse of fine and cool. Reversal **f** + **fan** = **cool**	**NAFF**
7	Hood's resort few <u>disturbed</u>. **Hoods resort few***	**SHERWOOD FOREST**
8	<u>Fantastic crowd</u> puller? Not half! **Crowd puller***	**WORLD CUP**
9	Is a bit less <u>wobbly</u>. **is a bit less***	**STABILISES**
10	Activity of person <u>hanging round</u> races? **TT** in **being**	**BETTING**

DOUBLE DEFINITION CLUES

1	Try Morse.	**ENDEAVOUR (as Insp. Morse)**
2	Units working for the queen.	**OHMS**
3	House team.	**VILLA (Aston V)**
4	Fully extended, eventually.	**AT LENGTH**
5	Sound like hounds, or one of the horses.	**BAY**
6	Punishment that ends with a period in the US.	**SENTENCE**
7	Fail to fill out Conference form?	**GO PEAR-SHAPED**
8	Made out to be important.	**DISTINGUISHED**
9	Psychiatrist's contract.	**SHRINK**
10	Detached supplement to a will.	**AWAY (when there's a will)**

CRYPTIC DEFINITION CLUES

1	Stored in it all the letters one writes.	**ALPHABET**
2	Beat with hands raised?	**OUTVOTE**
3	Sheet anchor.	**PAPERWEIGHT**
4	It may be said to limit one's drinking supply.	**WHEN (say when)**
5	They check wheels on their watches that have stopped.	**TRAFFIC WARDENS**
6	Mug presented at christening?	**BABY-FACE**

7	What's said to make controversy controversial?	**PRONUNCIATION**
8	Poles are put down by these Italians.	**GONDOLIERS**
9	Men that are sometimes moved to mate.	**CHESS PIECES**
10	Runs out of gas?	**VERBAL DIARRHOEA**

ADDITIVE CLUES

1	Development of fine photograph. **Of + f + shoot**	**OFFSHOOT**
2	Married to a Northerner - lucky thing! **M + a + Scot**	**MASCOT**
3	Vegetable presented with a dessert? That's a bloomer. **Sweet + pea**	**SWEET PEA**
4	FA present head of training. **Now + t**	**NOWT**
5	Bird left safe haven during flood. **L + ark**	**LARK**
6	Rented holiday home in very bad area. **v + ill + a**	**VILLA**
7	Dessert wines no great shakes. **Afters + hocks**	**AFTERSHOCKS**
8	Son having Indian food gets runs **S = son + curries**	**SCURRIES**
9	Hollywood's location causing a sensation all the time. **LA's tingly**	**LASTINGLY**
10	Wine-merchant's opening branches for Christmas in every area. **W + holly**	**SUNDER**

NOVELTY CLUES

1	Inappropriate comment of rugby player meeting queen.	**IMPROPER**
2	Pieces of chintz are ordered in this way - for wool it's the opposite. Letters in chintz are in alphabetic order	**ALPHABETIC**
3	Show dogs and horses. Point to pointers	**POINT-TO-POINTERS**

4	I can identify vehicles from here.	**ITALY**
	I = Italy (International Vehicle Registration)	
5	Appropriate payments for Henry James and Edward Lear?	**ROYALTIES**
	Kings and royal ties	
6	The tube fare.	**TV DINNER**
	Tube = TV	
7	Uproar caused by one line getting shifted in Europe's capitals.	**FURORE**
	Write EUROPE in capitals (sans serif) and move the bottom line in the first E over to the P	
8	Computer program suggesting neccesary changes?	**SPELLCHECKER**
	Neccesary should be necessary!	
9	Has had, for example, to make a change in this.	**TENSE**
	HAS and HAD different tenses	
10	If one cold toe is numb, two must be _____.	**EVEN NUMBER**
	Even more number	

3. Complete the clue – answers

	COMPLETE THE CLUE	SOLUTION
1	How long will you be?	**LIFESPAN**
2	Vote loser? Ridiculous!	**ROOSEVELT**
3	Root out heart of problem, and then do it again	**OBLITERATE**
4	Extreme break-out terrified guards	**UTTER**
5	SAD ain't present? Could be this worked?	**ANTI-DEPRESSANT**
6	What may show reduced waist measurement thanks to exercise?	**TAPE**
7	He looks as if he hasn't washed the back of his neck	**SCRUFF**
8	Test cricket is no diversion for boffin	**ROCKET SCIENTIST**

9	Complaint of plane passenger that may involve the handling of bags	**AIRSICKNESS**
10	Soldiers could make a military error crossing end of desert	**TERRITORIAL ARMY**
11	Instructions for enjoying cigarette at start of day	**FIRST LIGHT**
12	Where there may be a requirement for prior expertise, working inside	**MONASTERY**
13	Send lifers to stir for solitary	**FRIENDLESS**
14	Theatre opus possibly drawing in millions	**THE MOUSE TRAP**
15	These folk one's sort	**THE LIKES OF**
16	A drier's hers when working	**HAIRDRESSER**
17	Topless woman of ill-repute getting pulled at Northern club	**LUTON TOWN**
18	A chap could attend this celebration but never does	**STAG PARTY**
19	Great Dane is barking in open-air restaurant	**TEA GARDEN**
20	Square leg is bowler's target	**NINEPIN**
21	One way to get face relaxed	**LAIDBACK**
22	Meal eaten up	**HIGH TEA**
23	Barrow – place in which there's quiet estate, perhaps	**PUSHCART**
24	Generous firm leaving barrister to seek information	**UNSELFISH**
25	Something over my head – with no end of puzzlement, I finally get it!	**AHA**
26	Riots ruined most of course! It makes you spit!	**ROTISSERIE**
27	Poetic device exemplified in Keats and Yeats	**EYE-RHYME**
28	Who might show a sort of elitist learning?	**INTELLIGENTSIA**
29	River in old Bath turned out an apt place to live	**HOUSEBOAT**
30	Banker blocking account receives backing	**CERT**

4. Puzzles to try – annotated solutions

Each set displays the clue type in bold, the definitions in *italics* and the indicators <u>underlined</u>.

Practice Puzzle 1:

Across

2   *Calm down*, if <u>breaking</u> fast (6)
    Sandwich
    PACIFY – if in pacy
4   One medicine briefly <u>held back</u> in *large-scale health emergency* (8)
    Sandwich including **reversal** and **abbreviation**
    EPIDEMIC – I med. Reversed in epic
10 *Fruit* pie, originally, <u>cooked with</u> last pear (4-5)
    Anagram including **abbreviation**
    STAR-APPLE – (p(ie) last pear)*
11 *Device* of American providing private health care? (5)
    Novelty
    GISMO – GI's Med. Officer
12 *For Japanese ceremony, leaves much to be desired?* (3)
    Cryptic definition
    TEA
13 *Fiscal policy* making <u>Americans go wrong?</u> (11)
    Anagram
    REAGANOMICS – (Americans go)*
14 *Pickled* and *preserved in containers* (6)
    Double definition
    CANNED
16 <u>Said</u> completely to understand *Pope's position* (4,3)
    Additive including **homophone**
    HOLY SEE – wholly + see
19 *Cunning method to make an entrance, perhaps* (7)
    Additive
    ARCHWAY – arch + way
20 *Rocket* can make one scared, first <u>going off</u> (6)
    Take away
    EARFUL – (f)earful
22 *He collects a lot*, though record is <u>held by</u> worker (11)
    Sandwich
    ANTHOLOGIST – tho log is in ant
25 Old Man River is a *standard* (3)
    Additive including **abbreviation**
    PAR – pa + r
26 *Give up beef* (5)
    Double definition
    CHUCK
27 <u>Wrong</u> choice by opener in *sport* (3,6)
    Additive including **anagram**
    ICE HOCKEY – choice* + key
28 *Left* section <u>in</u> legal document (8)
    Sandwich
    DEPARTED – part in deed
29 *Operator of late ferry* running daily, initially (6)
    Additive
    CHARON – char + on

Down

1   *Money* <u>some</u> in Europe set aside (6)
    Hidden
    PESETA – Europe set aside
2   <u>Almost</u> risk <u>carrying</u> horse in *vehicle* (9)
    Sandwich including **take away**
    CHARABANC – Arab in chanc(e)
3   *Brilliance*, and what produces it, <u>say</u> (5)
    Homophone
    FLAIR – flare
5   *Group of artists* in rebuilt atelier, perhaps (3-11)
    Anagram
    PRE-RAPHAELITES – (rebuilt atelier)*

6 Follow and arrest *part of religious outfit* (3,6)
Additive
DOG COLLAR – dog + collar

7 *People* found as I'm <u>heading North</u>, <u>having crossed</u> South Africa? (5)
Sandwich including **reversal** and **abbreviation**
MASAI – SA in I am reversed

8 *Monastic life* is <u>embraced by</u> dimwit with hesitation (8)
Sandwich
CLOISTER – is in clot + er

9 *Getting higher in class?* <u>That could make one oddly</u> proud – and will, maybe (8,6)
Anagram
UPWARDLY MOBILE – (proud + will maybe)*

15 Recent delivery of *humorous magazine* (3,6)
Additive

NEW YORKER – new + yorker

17 In *game of cards*, one who punches the boss? (4,5)
Novelty
STUD POKER

18 Cavalryman's equipment <u>kept in</u> rotten *stable* (8)
Sandwich
BALANCED – lance in bad

21 Carbon material, as *alternative to charcoal* (6)
Additive including **abbreviation**
CRAYON – C + rayon

23 *Surpass - blast!* (5)
Double definition
TRUMP

24 *Old-fashioned loyalty* of Communist husband (5)
Additive including **abbreviation**
TROTH – Trot + h

....

Practice Puzzle 2:

Across

1 Brute roams wild in *botanical gardens* (10)
Anagram
ARBORETUMS – brute roams*

6 *Complain* vehicle has very little power (4)
Additive including **abbreviation**
CARP – car + p

9 *Shiny coat*, note, mislaid when touring part of Europe (5,5)
Additive including **abbreviation** and **sandwich**
GLOSS PAINT – G + Spain in lost

10 Half-heartedly catch single *fish* (4)
Additive
HOKI – ho(o)k + i

12 British PC having to face the music – that's *novel* (8,4)
Additive including **abbreviation**
BRIGHTON ROCK – B + right-on + rock

15 Went off, crossing river west of American city (9)
Additive including **sandwich** and **abbreviation**
ROTTERDAM – r in rotted + Am

17 Loiter about, wasting time in *bay* (5)
Take away including **abbreviation**
ORIEL – loiter* minus t

18 *Court official*, one <u>mediating between</u> councillor and monarch (5)
Sandwich including **abbreviations**
CRIER – I in Cr & ER

19 Information I've <u>circulated</u> to one woman and *another* (9)
Additive including **reversal**
GENEVIEVE – gen + I've reversed + Eve

20 France-gites: <u>new organisation</u> raking in pounds for <u>such a holiday</u>? (4-8)
Anagram including **sandwich** and **abbreviation**
SELF-CATERING – L in France-gites*

24 *Beastly noise* emanating from *zoo in Kenya* (4)
   Hidden
   OINK – zoo in Kenya
25 I will say a number of times: *twenty-seven?* (10)
   Additive
   ILLITERATE – I'll iterate
26 *Home* established at end of garden? (4)
   Semi all-in-one
   NEST – n + est
27 *Poorly educated and characterless?* (10)
   Cryptic definition
   UNLETTERED

Down
1 Sailor heading off on journey in *ship* (4)
   Additive including **take away**
   ARGO – (t)ar + go
2 Generous, keeping nothing in *personal account* (4)
   Sandwich including **abbreviation**
   BIOG – o in big
3 *Lowest possible cost* of jam and cereal for Spooner (7,5)
   Novelty
   RESERVE PRICE – preserve rice, a Spoonerism
4 *Accent in The Sound of Music?* (5)
   Cryptic definition
   TWANG
5 *Tom Thumb was a fighter* (9)
   Double definition
   MINUTEMAN

7 *Was sorry* a game plan ultimately proved deficient, when drawn up (10)
   Additive including **take away** and **reversal**
   APOLOGISED – a polo + desig(n) reversed
8 Old man's ailing more having swallowed liquid *form of medicine* (10)
   Additive including **sandwich**
   PAIN KILLER – ink in Pa iller
11 First of novices that is entering in nunnery is *troublesome* (12)
   Sandwich including **abbreviations**
   INCONVENIENT – n ie in convent
13 *Eventually finds line's out of action* (6,4)
   Double definition
   TRACKS DOWN – tracks down
14 Removes skin around fish for *youngsters* (10)
   Sandwich
   STRIPLINGS – ling in strips
16 Appreciate European renouncing a *drug* (9)
   Additive including **take away**
   DIGITALIN – dig + Italian less a
21 *Lift* beams, say (5)
   Homophone
   RAISE – rays
22 *Where you'll hear loud song?* (4)
   All-in-one
   FAIR – f + air
23 *Absolutely dull* (4)
   Double definition
   DEAD

....

Practice Puzzle 3:

Across
1 *Crash* impact something that's cut and dried (3,3,3)
   Additive
   HIT THE HAY – hit + the hay

6 *Warning* when about to miss bend in road (5)
   Take away
   AMBER – Camber = bend in road minus C = about

9 Be busy <u>with</u> part of kitchen *routine* (7)
   Additive
   HUMDRUM - hum = be busy + drum
   = part of kitchen
   (percussion instruments in orchestra)
10 Doctor repeating notes <u>about</u> one's
   tummy (7)
   Sandwich
   MIDRIFF - I in MD riff = repeating
   notes
11 Hammer <u>had no</u> time for this *director*
   (5)
   Take away
   MALLE - Mallet = hammer minus t =
   time
12 Bridge club <u>coming first</u> getting *medal*
   (4,5)
   Additive
   IRON CROSS - iron = club + cross =
   bridge (verb)
14 *Claim interest* (3)
   Double definition
   BAG - bag in sense of 'not my bag'
15 *Inflated* hydrogen in hut failing to
   <u>explode</u> (11)
   Sandwich
   HIGHFALUTIN - H = hydrogen in
   anag. hut failing
17 *Means* to <u>fill</u> crew here with alarm (11)
   Hidden
   WHEREWITHAL
19 *Yob* one <u>encountered in</u> fair (3)
   Sandwich
   OIK - I = one in OK = fair (N.B. with a
   question-mark at the end this would
   have been a **semi all-in-one**)
20 *Opposition parties* accordingly
   <u>gathering</u> call for leader <u>to go</u> (4,3,2)
   Sandwich
   THEM AND US - Demand minus D in
   thus = accordingly
22 Exercise <u>noisily</u> in *ancient woodland* (5)
   Homophone
   WEALD
24 Stranger <u>stopping</u> helps <u>foreign</u> girl (7)
   Sandwich
   ELSPETH - ET = stranger (Spielberg
   movie) in anag. helps

26 In the distance lie <u>back</u>, lapping up
   the cream (7)
   Sandwich
   ELITISM - indicated by in inc.
   reversal indicated by back
27 Irish politician that I <u>got involved in</u>
   firm (5)
   Sandwich
   TONED - One = I in TD = Irish
   politician (abbrev. for Teachta Dala)
26 *Reason for body appearing in fracas?*
   (5,4)
   Sandwich
   RIFLE SHOT - Flesh = body in riot =
   fracas. This clue is also **all-in-one** as
   the whole sentence leads to the
   solution without a clear definition.

Down
1 *That's boring* old Henry interrupting
   Cardinal <u>endlessly</u> (2,3)
   Sandwich including **take away**
   HO-HUM - O = old H = henry in
   HUM(E) = Cardinal
2 Miss broadcast after <u>mounting</u> *delay*
   (4,3)
   Reversal
   TIME LAG - Gal = miss emit =
   broadcast both reversed
3 *Base metal* <u>forged</u> from pieces in Soho
   and SE25 (9)
   Anagram
   HORSESHOE - anag. fodder Soho SE
   & her (from 25 down solution)
4 Lass giving off smell, *one hanging in
   the air* (11)
   Novelty
   HUMMINGBIRD - humming bird =
   smelly girl
5 <u>Lift</u> part of spring *vegetable plant* (3)
   Reversal
   YAM - May reversed
6 Like detectives <u>turning up</u> old
   detection method (5)
   Additive including **reversal**
   ASDIC - As + reversed CID

7 *Rescue* from trouble <u>in</u> fight (4,3)
Sandwich
BAIL OUT - Ail = trouble in bout = fight

8 *Dissident* caught <u>escaping from</u> jail after scrap (9)
Additive including **take away**
REFUSENIK - Refuse = scrap + nick minus c

13 *A spinster no longer immediately available* (3-3-5)
Double definition
OFF-THE-SHELF - c.f. on the shelf

14 Caves in time <u>swallowing</u> trunk *road in city* (3,6)
Sandwich
BOW STREET - Tree = trunk in bows = caves in plus t = time

16 *Innocent* one they will <u>corrupt</u> (4-5)
Anagram
LILY-WHITE - of I they will indicated by corrupt

18 *Poet's* green: <u>not</u> a lord but boy (7)
Additive including **take away**
EMERSON - Emerald less a ld (= a Lord) + son = boy

19 Nothing wrong with one having a hard *book* (7)
Additive
OBADIAH - o = nothing + bad = wrong + I = one + a h = hard

21 Odd characters from MASH met and taken away *in van* (5)
Hidden
AHEAD - Alternately hidden in even letters of MASH met and

23 *Resign* from French-American college (5)
Additive
DEMIT - de = from in French + MIT = American college (Massachusetts Institute of Technology)

25 Man <u>not</u> born *of woman* (3)
Take away
HER - Herb less b = born

....

Practice Puzzle 4:

Across

1 *Act outrageously*, putting a minute hole <u>in</u> trophy (4,2,2)
Sandwich
CAMP IT UP - a m pit in cup

9 <u>Lacking</u> energy, a race with axes gets you *fit* (8)
Additive including **take away**
APOPLEXY - a p(e)ople + x,y (axis)

10 *Ideal conditions*, with plump old woman <u>hugging</u> one! (6)
Sandwich
OPTIMA - I in opt + ma

11 <u>Covering</u> duck a weakness with some cricket *commentaries* (5-5)
Sandwich
VOICE-OVERS - o in vice + overs

12 <u>Pronounced</u> fit, *he was done in before anyone else* (4)
Homophone
ABEL - able

13 *Hard* to admire kid getting old (4,5-1)
Additive
LIKE BILLY-O - like + Billy (the Kid) + O

16 *Event* broadcast live <u>in</u> the New Year? (7)
Sandwich including **anagram**
JAVELIN - live* in Jan

17 *Where you'll find something burning in range?* (7)
All-in-one
KITCHEN - itch in ken

20 *Intense campaign* settled <u>audience's</u> worries <u>reflected</u> in petition (10)
Sandwich including **reversal** and **homophone**
BLITZKRIEG - litz + irks = irkz reversed in beg

22 *One in exaltation* left couples venue (4)
Additive
LARK - l + ark (exaltation of larks)

23 Weaving till Lent keeps the French or
   Spanish *orphan in work* (6,4)
   Sandwich including **anagram**
   LITTLE NELL – le or el in (till lent)*
   orphan in *The Old Curiosity Shop*
25 With it, legal document is *beyond
   doubt* (6)
   Additive
   INDEED – in = 'with it' + DEED
26 Succeeded in moving cables following
   shower of pitch (4,4)
   Sandwich including **anagram**
   BASS CLEF – s in cables* + f
27 Round Britain spikes discovered
   hidden in *pea soup?* (8)
   Sandwich
   FOGBOUND – O GB in found

Down

2 A postgrad conceals lie spoken by one
   in *biology class* (8)
   Sandwich including **homophone**
   AMPHIBIA – A + fib = phib I in MA
3 Rests under haystack, in part with
   most needles? (10)
   Sandwich
   PRICKLIEST – rick lies in pt
4 A stickler for recycling bottles very
   green on transport (6-4)
   Sandwich including **anagram**
   TRAVEL-SICK – v in (a stickler)*
5 *Dreadfully anxious* to include a name
   in particular (7)
   Sandwich
   PANICKY – a n in picky
6 *Came to* two Kensington houses (4)
   Hidden
   WOKE – two Kensington

7 *Happened* to live with doctor I didn't
   like (6)
   Additive
   BEFELL – be + (I do not love thee,
   Doctor) Fell
8 *Be prepared for a possible house call!*
   (4,4)
   Cryptic definition
   EYES DOWN – bingo reference
14 Twin brothers hiding leading couple's
   expensive jewellery (5-5)
   Additive including **take away**
   BLING BLING – (si)bling (si)bling
15 Little room to embrace radical reform
   in *regional service* (5,5)
   Sandwich including **anagram**
   LOCAL RADIO – radical* in loo
16 *People hope to be placed on their
   membership lists* (3,5)
   Cryptic definition
   JOB CLUBS – CD ref. 'being placed' =
   getting a job.
18 *Pole, perhaps,* Scotsman stuffed with
   cord (8)
   Sandwich
   EUROPEAN – rope in Euan
19 Compromise on deferred *issue* (4,3)
   Additive
   GIVE OFF – give = compromise + off
   = deferred
21 *Question in it is in Latin?* (2,4)
   All-in-one
   IQ TEST – Q in it + est
24 *Girl*, thoroughly English, from the
   South (4)
   Reversal
   ELLA – all E reversed

Practice Puzzle 5:

Across

1 Great bloke on pole, *the main
   controller* (8)
   Additive including **abbreviation**
   STOPCOCK – S + top cock

6 *Where schoolchildren snitch?* (6)
   Cryptic definition
   INFORM – in form

9 Workers in need of answer get *the last word* (4)
Additive including **abbreviation**
AMEN – a + men

10 Strange feeling a bit attached to one, beginning to eulogise shoe! (10)
Additive including **abbreviation**
ESPADRILLE – ESP + a drill + e

11 *A prickly thing* to go without God among Britain's extremists (10)
BLACKTHORN – lack Thor in B(ritai)n

13 Test a number of groups in biology (4)
Additive
TAXA – tax + a

14 German reversed round a vehicle, *it's plain to see* (8)
Sandwich including **reversal**
SAVANNAH – a van in Hans reversed

16 *Emphasise why off work?* (6)
Double definition
STRESS

18 Poor dog! Not many get *restraining order* (6)
Additive
CURFEW – cur + few

20 *Might etrol be?* (4-4)
Novelty
LEAD-FREE – petrol less first letter = lead

22 *Dairy product* needs wife to call for attention (4)
Additive including **abbreviation**
WHEY – w + hey

24 High cost of living holds single relative back (10)
Sandwich including **abbreviation** and **reversal**
EXORBITANT – I bro(ther) reversed in extant

26 Wine has colour which is *superior to body* (10)
Additive
GRAVESTONE – Graves + tone

28 *Prime minister is in the garden* (4)
Double definition
EDEN

29 Fancy fish *to sell down the river* (6)
Additive
BETRAY – bet + ray

30 Cryptic finished, *as you'd expect one to be?* (8)
Anagram
FIENDISH – finished*

Down

2 I'm an adult wandering in *state bordering Kerala* (5,4)
Anagram
TAMIL NADU – (I'm an adult)*

3 Wok expert given a *comprehensive fix* (7)
Additive
PANACEA – pan + ace + a

4 *Open* delivering Carnoustie's fifth green (5)
Additive including **abbreviation**
OVERT – O + vert

5 *Football stand* quiet after start of game (3)
Additive including **abbreviations**
KOP – KO + p

6 One's in the subcontinent – *north-west of here?* (9)
Sandwich
INDONESIA – one's in India

7 Hot food, so blow (7)
Double definition
FRITTER

8 King, having captured US city, *put feet up* (5)
Sandwich including **abbreviation**
RELAX – LA in Rex

12 *Play*: it starts 'In the beginning' by word of introduction (7)
Additive including **abbreviation**
OTHELLO – OT + hello

15 *What's needed when jumper in such a state?* (3,6)
Cryptic definition
NEW JERSEY

17 Southern bird over promontory – *serious nature!* (9)
Additive
STERNNESS – S + tern + ness

19 *The High Road*, where insect settled (7)
Additive
FLYOVER – fly over
21 *Charlie* seeks articles <u>in</u> fashion (7)
Sandwich
FATHEAD – the a in fad
23 *Might one be up on this drug?* (5)
Cryptic definition
HORSE

25 Note always <u>turning up</u> – *rare one?* (5)
Reversal
BREVE – ever B reversed
27 *Is his brain left <u>redundant</u>?* (3)
All-in-one
OAF – loaf less l

....

Practice Puzzle 6:

Across
1 Fast vehicle ahead is *a hardtop* (8)
Additive
CARAPACE – car + apace
5 *Assorted pieces* (6)
All-in-one anagram
SPECIE – pieces*
9 Son having Indian food gets *runs* (8)
Additive
SCURRIES – s + curries
10 *Prevents further development of hair-raising exploits* (6)
Double definition
STUNTS
12 Writer is available in a foreign edition, *pirated* (12)
Sandwich
UNAUTHORISED – author is in un Ed
15 *Entertainment* of old a theatre company <u>rejected</u> (5)
Additive including **reversal** and **abbreviation**
OPERA – o + a rep reversed
16 *Sudden descent downhill* makes skier <u>tremble</u> with cold (9)
Anagram
ROCKSLIDE – (skier + cold)*
18 Mostly prevent men <u>going round</u> old *part of theatre* (5,4)
Sandwich
STAGE DOOR – aged in sto(p) or
19 *Type of mushroom* used in casserole? No kidding (5)
Hidden
ENOKI – casserole no kidding

20 French composer almost worth *considering* (12)
Additive including **take away**
DELIBERATING – Delibe(s) + rating
24 Finally decide between right and wrong *answer* (6)
Sandwich including **abbreviations**
RETORT – e in r + tort
25 A holm oak's <u>rotten</u> *state* (8)
Anagram
OKLAHOMA – (a holm oak)*
26 Issue <u>about</u> getting sister accommodated in *pleasant property* (3,3)
Sandwich including **abbreviation** and **reversal**
DES RES – sr in seed reversed
27 *Student*, proud to secure a first in divinity at university (8)
Sandwich including **abbreviations**
GRADUAND – a d U in grand

Down
1 *Performers* in stage musical, <u>giving a twirl at the end</u> (4)
Letter shift
CAST – cats
2 Bitter herb <u>said</u> to make *sauce base* (4)
Homophone
ROUX – rue
3 *Ancestors* are not <u>recorded</u> in part of book (9)
Sandwich including **abbreviation**
PARENTAGE – aren't in page

4 A-level body must support oral examiner: *it's laid out in black and white* (12)
Additive including **homophone**
CHEQUERBOARD – checker + board

6 *Old man's* half-hearted talk (5)
Take away
PATER – pa(t)ter

7 Working on mini-cars for *stars* (5,5)
Anagram
CANIS MINOR – (on mini-cars)*

8 *Be careful* of morally suspect female's charm (4,4,2)
Additive
EASY DOES IT – easy + doe's + it

11 *Drama* teacher's unusual interpretation meets resistance (3,9)
Additive including **anagram** and **abbreviation**
THE CARETAKER – teacher* + take + r

13 *Thought about* assigning right and left wingers to team (10)
Sandwich
CONSIDERED – side in Con + red

14 Woman's account inflamed American *philosopher* (10)
Additive including **abbreviations**
HERACLITUS – her + ac lit + US

17 Employee on board <u>keeps</u> sailors *near rear of ship* (9)
Sandwich including **abbreviation**
STERNWARD – RN in steward

21 *Lighter* piece of metal, say, <u>can be lifted</u> (5)
Additive including **reversal** and **abbreviation**
BARGE – bar + eg reversed

22 *US state* <u>initiating</u> investigation of Watergate aftermath (4)
Letter selection
IOWA – i + o + w + a

23 Given accommodation in flat, *I settled* (4)
Sandwich
PAID – I in pad

···

Practice Puzzle 7:

Across

1 Mates <u>heading off</u> to fantastic *part of France* (6)
Additive including **take away**
ALSACE – pals less p + ace

4 A boy <u>tucked into</u> grain, *having added salt* (8)
Sandwich
SEASONED – a son in seed

10 *Bird* or rock rabbit? (9)
Additive
STONECHAT – stone + chat

11 *Sign* off, say, <u>when retiring</u> (5)
Additive including **abbreviation** and **reversal**
BADGE – bad + eg reversed

12 Slight suspicion fish <u>ejected</u> *liquid* (3)
Take away
INK – inkling less ling

13 *Has second thoughts about* conditions in which English politicians <u>are kept</u> (11)
Additive including **sandwich** and **abbreviation**
RECONSIDERS – E Cons in riders

14 *I eat spinach* and fish you served (6)
Additive
POPEYE – pope + ye

16 *Female* rider <u>falls during</u> dressage, <u>losing heart</u> (7)
Sandwich including **anagram** and **take away**
DEIRDRE – rider* in d(ressag)e

19 One part of the Bible: part of the Old Testament, *actually* (2,5)
Additive including **abbreviations**
IN TRUTH – I + NT + Ruth

20 <u>To members of audience</u>, players sounded *fed up* (6)
Homophone
SIGHED - side

22 *Unable to manoeuvre forty gallons or so?* (4,1,6)
Double definition
OVER A BARREL

25 Male loves *unpopular woman* (3)
Additive including **abbreviation**
MOO - m + o o

26 *After start of* offensive, soldiers leave <u>distant region</u> (5)
Additive including **abbreviation**
OTAGO - O + TA + go

27 *Discussion of NHS care?* (9)
Cryptic definition
TREATMENT

28 *Reserve* little time <u>for visiting</u> holiday resort (3,5)
Sandwich including **abbreviation**
SET ASIDE - t in seaside

29 *Language* suppressed by anger management (6)
Hidden
GERMAN - anger management

Down

1 *Engineer* using gold — <u>singular</u> kind of metal (6)
Additive including **abbreviations**
AUSTIN - Au + s tin

2 *Place* to store wine (9)
Additive
STOCKPORT - stock port

3 *Food and drink* down in price – dropping a penny (5)
Take away including **abbreviation**
CHEER - cheaper less a p

5 Daughter <u>restricted by rare</u> digestion trouble ... *having this?* (6,8)
Sandwich including **anagram**
EATING DISORDER - d in (digestion trouble)*

6 Minor railway track *sinking into the ground* (9)
Additive
SUBSIDING - sub + siding

7 *Jog* with no clothes on and you'll get good <u>hiding</u> (5)
Sandwich including **abbreviation**
NUDGE - g in nude

8 *Island's judge* put off <u>accepting</u> European finance system (8)
Sandwich including **abbreviation**
DEEMSTER - EMS in deter

9 *Yellow* and red suit <u>briefly worn by</u> fashionable fellows (7-7)
Sandwich including **take away**
CHICKEN-HEARTED - heart(s) in chic Ken + Ed

15 *Trainers* <u>sorted out</u> our cadets (9)
Anagram
EDUCATORS - (our cadets)*

17 Fancy a drink with meal <u>to begin with?</u> *The perfect combination* (5,4)
Additive including **abbreviation**
DREAM TEAM - dream + tea + m

18 Tailless mousy trio <u>scurries about</u> *showing fear* (8)
Anagram including **take away**
TIMOROUS - (mous(y) trio)*

21 *Dumpling* puts weight on - a lot of weight! (6)
Additive including **abbreviation**
WONTON - w on + ton

23 *Demand* divorcee put before a court (5)
Additive including **abbreviation**
EXACT - ex + a ct

24 Piece of wood placed on <u>end of</u> the *artisan's machine* (5)
Additive including **abbreviation**
LATHE - lath + e

Practice Puzzle 8:

Across

1 A revolutionary plan <u>going round</u> *the educational community* (8)
Additive including **reversal**
ACADEMIA - a + Cade + aim reversed

6 <u>So-called</u> person beating *the booze* (6)
Homophone
LIQUOR - licker

9 <u>Characters involved</u> in Shakespearean *plot* (4)
Hidden
AREA - Shakespearean

10 *What pyromaniac must do furiously* (4,6)
Double definition
LIKE BLAZES

11 *Very, very good standard not welcomed in the main* (5,5)
Cryptic definition
JOLLY ROGER

13 Give spanking good *smack* (4)
Additive including **abbreviation**
TANG - tan + g

14 Pain and misfortune - yet *one remains optimistic* (8)
Additive
PANGLOSS - pang + gloss

16 *Offensive* radio <u>broadcast about</u> noon (6)
Sandwich including **anagram**
INROAD - n in radio*

18 Dash <u>outside</u> with *criminal* (6)
Sandwich
BANDIT - and in bit

20 What may be drunk by a politician is *dependent on chance* (8)
Additive
ALEATORY - ale + a Tory

22 *Successfully secures a great deal* (4)
Double definition
BAGS

24 *Craft needed by person with failing party?* (3-7)
Cryptic definition
ICE-BREAKER

26 *Ecstasy* obtained from him servant <u>adulterated</u> (10)
Anagram
RAVISHMENT - (him servant)*

28 *Romantic couple's bit of news* (4)
Double definition
ITEM

29 *Crowning moment* of the second of 'Three Men In A Boat' (6)
Additive
HEIGHT - h + eight

30 *Ruin* song with one dance move that's <u>not</u> quiet (3,5)
Additive including **take away** and **abbreviation**
LAY WASTE - lay + w + a + ste(p)

Down

2 Diamonds are real, asked initially? *Sauce!* (9)
Additive including **abbreviation**
CARBONARA - carbon + a = are + r + a

3 *Suffering from a number of blows* (4,3)
Cryptic definition
DEAD LEG

4 *Cheeky* madam <u>finally moves to the front</u> in panic (5)
Letter shift
MALAR - alarm with m moved

5 Article written on British *diver* (3)
Additive
AUK - a + UK

6 *His policy*: <u>carrying</u> one to bed when husband's <u>away</u>? (9)
Sandwich including **take away** and **abbreviation**
LIBERTINE - I + bert(h) in line

7 Somewhere to live <u>down</u> south for *three months* (7)
Take away including **abbreviation**
QUARTER - quarter(s)

8 Duck is able <u>to cross</u> Eastern *Pacific* (5)
Sandwich including **abbreviation**
OCEAN - O + E in can

12 *See red* after game's over (2,5)
   Additive
   GO SPARE – go + spare
15 *Tell me quickly* what's unfashionable and fashionable! (3,4,2)
   Additive
   OUT WITH IT – out + with it
17 A welcome home for chaps <u>in</u> *union* (9)
   Sandwich
   AGREEMENT – men in a greet
19 *Striking as blade might be* (7)
   Double definition
   DASHING
21 *A Catherine* that had Sinatra <u>smitten</u>? (7)
   Anagram
   TSARINA – Sinatra*

23 *Saying* of Lovelace, say, has <u>turned up</u> (5)
   Additive including **reversal** and **abbreviation**
   ADAGE – Ada + eg reversed
25 <u>Upsetting</u> salt over turkey <u>wings</u> could make one *cross* (5)
   Additive including **reversal** and **take away**
   RATTY – tar reversed + t(urke)y
27 *Fish* given in list (<u>after</u> horse) (3)
   Take away including **abbreviation**
   EEL – h + eel

....

Practice Puzzle 9:

Across

1 First fop <u>prepared</u> *to go naked?* (5,3)
   Anagram
   STRIP OFF – (first fop)*
5 *Advise* what Pam needs to take pain (6)
   Letter shift
   INFORM – Pam with in for m
9 *Way of bowling done deviously through cover* (9)
   Double definition
   UNDERHAND
11 *Send to specialist*, concerned with iron reading <u>barely showing</u> (5)
   Additive including **abbreviation**
   REFER – re + Fe + r(eading)
12 Church father's <u>returning</u> hot *treasure* (7)
   Additive including **abbreviation** and **reversal**
   CHERISH – Ch + sire reversed + h
13 Confining to school <u>involves</u> Rugby's head *being harsh* (7)
   Sandwich including **abbreviation**
   GRATING – r in gating

14 Prestige owner <u>arranged for</u> *help in driving* (5,8)
   Anagram
   POWER STEERING – (prestige owner)*
16 We pot blue – shot's <u>complicated</u> and *very involved* (2,2,3,6)
   Anagram
   UP TO THE ELBOWS – (we pot blue shot)*
20 *What will have character <u>shortly</u> immersed in here?* (7)
   All-in-one including **take away**
   SMOKING – kind less d in smog
21 *Good-natured?* A fine story (7)
   Additive including **abbreviation**
   AFFABLE – a f fable
23 Cleaner's put marks on *small ornament* (5)
   Additive including **abbreviation**
   CHARM – char + m
24 *Cutting* fish <u>without</u> right article takes time (9)
   Sandwich including **abbreviations**
   TRENCHANT – r in tench an t

25 Ultimately right to be agitated when son's gone missing – *as a small child will do* (6)
Additive including **abbreviation** and **take away**
TEETHE – (righ)t + (s)eethe

26 With complete year's *guarantee* (8)
Additive including **abbreviations**
WARRANTY – w + arrant + y

Across

1 *Artificial channel* cut across middle of obstruction (6)
Sandwich including **abbreviation**
SLUICE – u in slice

2 British leaving to make way across *watershed...* (5)
Take away including **abbreviation**
RIDGE – bridge less B

3 *...experience range* with almost unlimited vista (7)
Additive including **take away**
PURVIEW – pur(e) + view

4 What's great about obese woman chasing achievement as *a boxer* (13)
Additive
FEATHERWEIGHT – feat + her weight

6 *Tell* managed to get up speed (7)
Additive including **reversal**
NARRATE – ran reversed + rate

7 *Where boundaries must have been crossed* if film's to get broadcast (3-6)
Anagram
OFF-LIMITS – (if film's to)*

8 Tons keep quiet when entering into extra *borrowing arrangement* (8)
Sandwich including **abbreviation**
MORTGAGE – (t + gag) in more

10 *What's made only to snap in bits?* (7,6)
Cryptic definition
DIGITAL CAMERA

14 *Sponsorship* scrapped for pageant that lacks following (9)
Anagram including **take away**
PATRONAGE – (for pageant)* less f

15 *Tom perhaps asked what's new in camera* (8)
Double definition
PUSSYCAT – movie

17 Perhaps play from another suit over hearts, securing one *win* (7)
Sandwich including **abbreviation**
TRIUMPH – I in trump + h

18 *Policeman* in charge in bid for acceptance (7)
Sandwich including **abbreviation**
OFFICER – ic in offer

19 *Somewhere in church* match shortly is concluded with lines (6)
Additive including **take away**
VESTRY – vest(a) + Ry

22 *This is strong meat* (5)
Double definition
BRAWN

....

Practice Puzzle 10:

Across

1 *Stonework* produced by girl carrying child (7)
Sandwich
MASONRY – son in Mary

5 *African* – his room needs refurbishment (7)
Anagram
MOORISH – (his room)*

9 *Put up* with limit after I left for university (9)
Novelty
CONSTRUCT – U for I in constrict

10 *Tool* causing *a sudden problem* (5)
Double definition
FACER

11 American serviceman <u>sent back</u> to
smallest room in *White House* (5)
Additive including **reversal**
IGLOO – GI rev + loo

12 Gordon led <u>astray</u>, making *a bloomer* (9)
Anagram
GOLDEN ROD – (Gordon led)*

13 *Some drivers do remain inconspicuous*
(4,1,4,4)
Double definition
TAKE A BACK SEAT

17 Dispatched to island, people
correspond *in mawkish fashion* (13)
Additive including **abbreviation**
SENTIMENTALLY – sent + I + men +
tally

21 Vamp is <u>about</u> to *reform*? On the
contrary (9)
Sandwich
IMPROVISE – is in improve

24 *Block off nearby cul-de-sac* (5)
Triple definition
CLOSE

25 *Endow* part of a hospital (5)
Additive
AWARD – a + ward

26 Love car <u>with top removed</u> for <u>holding</u>
party *in the open air* (3-2-4)
Sandwich including **take away**
OUT-OF-DOOR – O + (a)uto + do in for

27 *Showing impatience*, say, <u>going back
inside</u> too soon (7)
Sandwich including **abbreviation**
and **reversal**
EAGERLY – eg rev in early

28 Historian city's heard of (7)
Homophone
Carlyle – CARLISLE

Down

1 *Do one's share*, putting up with family
(6)
Additive including **reversal**
MUCK IN – cum rev + kin

2 Give information and reveal *just one
thing* (9)
Additive
SINGLETON – sing + let on

3 To *develop business contacts*, new
serviceman <u>has introduced</u> a couple (7)
Sandwich including **abbreviation**
NETWORK – two in n + erk

4 Racy rogue's <u>prepared</u> *address* (4,5)
Anagram
YOUR GRACE – (racy rogue)*

5 *Copper possibly* had an encounter <u>with</u>
gangster (5)
Additive
METAL – met + Al (Capone)

6 Out of condition, almost sickly-
looking – *but not in the rush hour* (3-4)
Additive including **take away**
OFF-PEAK – off + peak(y)

7 *Meet with* popular scoundrel (5)
Additive
INCUR – in + cur

8 They ride <u>out</u> to get *what's coming to
them* (8)
Anagram
HEREDITY – (they ride)*

14 *Genuine* article <u>accepted</u> by family
member in charge (9)
Sandwich including **abbreviation**
AUTHENTIC – the in aunt + i/c

15 <u>Confused?</u> Go to Ely, my *original
source* (9)
Anagram
ETYMOLOGY – (go to Ely my)*

16 *Stop* making reptile cross (8)
Additive
ASPIRATE – asp + irate

18 *Monks are suitable* (2,5)
Double definition
IN ORDER

19 *A match for Venus* (7)
Double definition
LUCIFER

20 *Step*, jade green, <u>worn away at edges</u> (6)
Take away
DEGREE – (ja)de gree(n)

22 Paramedics <u>initially</u> called *to crash* (5)
Additive including **abbreviation**
PRANG – P + rang

23 *Elemental sarcasm* (5)
Double definition
IRONY – of iron

Practice Puzzle 11:

Across

1 *Loudly criticises private housing* (8)
Double definition
BARRACKS

9 Brief *sound of glasses touching twice, when this is said?* (4-4)
All-in-one
CHIN-CHIN - chin(k) + chin(k)

10 *Man* confused by *events* (6)
Anagram
STEVEN - events*

11 Was initially unhappy to do a turn in farewell *show* (10)
Sandwich
VAUDEVILLE - lived + u reversed in vale

12 Barrel with top grade *fish* (4)
Additive
TUNA - tun + A

13 *It may result in another hearing*, on appeal (10)
Additive
REPETITION - re (= on) + petition (= appeal)

16 *Important match* played again after setback (7)
Reversal
DECIDER - re-diced reversed

17 *Soldier* or cadet has to be trained (7)
Anagram
REDCOAT - or cadet

20 *Done with wealth, possibly?* (4-2-4)
All-in-one anagram
DOWN-AT-HEEL - (done wealth)*

22 Oddly ignored sexy Greek *heroine* (4)
Alternately **hidden**
EYRE - (s)e(x)y(G)r(e)e(k)

23 Jailbird and group of scoundrels *showing no disagreement* (10)
Additive
CONCURRING - con + cur ring

25 *Upset*, wearing green (6)
Additive
INVERT - in + vert

26 One about to keep on fighting getting *weighty equipment* (8)
Sandwich
IRONWARE - on + war in I re

27 Naturally preserves *various items* (8)
Additive
SUNDRIES - sun dries

Down

2 *Pictures shown to audience here* (3,5)
Cryptic definition
ART HOUSE

3 *The last book* to give clergyman joy? (10)
Additive
REVELATION - rev + elation

4 Officer steps in to transform *meeting* (10)
Sandwich including **abbreviation**
CONVERGENT - Gen. in convert

5 Crowd at party with no stomach for *rough drink* (7)
Additive including **take away**
SCRUMPY - scrum + p(art)y

6 *Coal supplier makes a bomb* (4)
Double definition
MINE

7 After cold starter, I provided *hot dish* (6)
Additive
CHILLI - chill + I

8 Prisoner's short time to find *where PC gets information* (8)
Additive including **abbreviation**
INTERNET - interne + t

14 Go to inhale crack - it's *divine* (10)
Anagram
THEOLOGIAN - (go to inhale)*

15 *Kept going*, getting travel permit clipped at ferry port (6,4)
Additive including **take away**
TICKED OVER - ticke(t) + Dover

16 Had a role in charge *of teaching* (8)
Additive including **abbreviation**
DIDACTIC - did act + ic

18 Tune appropriate to church *service* (3,5)
   Additive including **abbreviation**
   AIR FORCE - air + for + CE
19 Say what inventor does for *town* (7)
   Homophone
   DEVIZES - devises

21 *Unrestrained* soldier conquered <u>all around</u>(6)
   Sandwich
   WANTON - ant in won
24 *Certainly no counterfeit coin* (4)
   Cryptic definition
   REAL

Practice Puzzle 12:

Across

1 *Bloom* lady-killer <u>put back in</u> buttonhole (10)
   Sandwich including **reversal**
   CORNFLOWER - wolf reversed in corner

6 *Pot for reheated meat and vegetables* (4)
   Double definition
   HASH

8 *Like young female* swimmer <u>saved by</u> male (8)
   Sandwich
   MAIDENLY - ide in manly

9 <u>When speaking</u>, made fun of a *group leader* (6)
   Homophone
   GUIDER - guyed a

10 Old soldiers <u>retreating</u>? *Captain brought to book* (4)
   Reversal including **abbreviation**
   NEMO - o + men all reversed

11 *Unexpected* pair <u>implicated</u> in US-<u>backed</u> insurgency (10)
   Sandwich including **reversal** and **abbreviation**
   SURPRISING - Pr in US (reversed) + rising

12 *Teacher's instruction after question's answered without effort* (5,4)
   Double definition
   HANDS DOWN

14 *Shows effect of strain in fights* (5)
   Double definition
   FRAYS

17 *Dog* <u>brought back</u> hares about <u>end of</u> hunt (5)
   Sandwich including **reversal** and **abbreviation**
   SPITZ - (hun)t in zips

19 *Not quite enough to make up two teams for a game* (6-3)
   Cryptic definition
   TWENTY-ONE

22 *Fascinating woman* jailed <u>after tussle about</u> love and deception (5,5)
   Sandwich including **anagram** and **abbreviation**
   JOLIE LAIDE - o + lie in jailed*

23 *German banker* <u>circulating</u> two notes (4)
   Reversal
   ODER - re do reversed

24 *Most appealing* version of film is French (6)
   Additive
   CUTEST - cut + est

25 *Undeveloped* island on which explorer <u>briefly</u> lands (8)
   Additive including **take away**
   INCHOATE - inch + Oate(s)

26 Unconscious immediately after <u>start of</u> boxing match (4)
   Additive including **abbreviation**
   BOUT - b + out

27 *Having moral principles*, objected to drunk being given precedence (4,6)
   Additive
   HIGH-MINDED - high + minded

Down

1 *American people* given care of <u>seventy percent</u> of city (9)
Additive including **abbreviation** and **take away**
COMANCHES - c/o + Manches(ter)

2 *They've made tracks* and left <u>wearing shortened</u> garments (7)
Sandwich including **abbreviation** and **take away**
RAILMEN - in raimen(t)

3 Lad dines <u>out</u> in *part of airport* (8)
Anagram
LANDSIDE - (lad dines)*

4 *Chant questioning restaurant staff's raison d'être?* (3,3,2,7)
Cryptic definition
WHY ARE WE WAITING

5 *Look for respect* (6)
Double definition
REGARD

6 *Top setter supplying solution* (9)
Double definition
HAIRSPRAY

7 Longing to have animals <u>raised</u> in *part of the capital* (7)
Reversal
STEPNEY - yen + pets all reversed

13 Easing of hostilities <u>ends prematurely</u> around border, resulting in *damage* (9)
Sandwich including **take away**
DETRIMENT - rim in detent(e)

15 <u>In various</u> parades ambassador's taken *lead* (9)
Sandwich including **anagram** and **abbreviation**
SPEARHEAD - HE in parades*

16 *Means of transmitting messages* <u>installed in</u> teleprinter commonly (8)
Hidden
INTERCOM - teleprinter commonly

18 Academic at university has little time for *penitent politician* (7)
Additive including **abbreviation**
PROFUMO - prof + U + mo

20 *Gothic script expert?* (3,4)
Cryptic definition
OLD HAND

21 Find *fault* with <u>endless</u> razzmatazz at church (6)
Additive including **abbreviation**
GLITCH - glit(z) + ch

5. Thanks and acknowledgements

Such is the enthusiasm for *The Times* Crossword that many good people volunteered to help me write this book; there were so many that I was unable to take up all the offers. It was Anne Bradford who was a prime mover and I thank her for that.

Nigel Broadbent (a musician friend and composer of a more artistic kind) encouraged me frequently, especially when I was stuck for quite a time.

Workshops for beginners have enabled me to test my ideas for the transfer of teaching from a course environment to the written word, and I am grateful to the contributions made by adult students at Marlborough College Summer School, Earnley Concourse, The Hill in Abergavenny and Farncombe Estate in the Cotswolds.

A former lecturing colleague, John Ambrose ('I'll never be able to do cryptic crosswords') was the guinea pig for the basics and offered some presentational ideas.

Long-time solvers Roy Dean, Erwin Hatch, Glynne Jones, Richard Morse and Paul Williams shared their solving techniques with me, as did newish solvers Lyn Packman and Jill Loveless, both former workshop participants.

The fairly recent appearance of internet comment on *The Times* Crossword has been well-timed; I have been able to tap into the views of the many bloggers. A number of the chosen clues were published as 'Clue of the Week' in *The Week* magazine, having been recommended to me by Paul Crossley, a regular *Times* and Mephisto solver.

My favourite setter, Brian Greer, allowed me to use clues from his earlier (out-of-print) book on *The Times* Crossword; and Colin Clarke, co-founder of the Gruntlings crossword group, as always gave me sound advice on tricky points.

Special thanks to Richard Heald, Erwin Hatch and Harvey Freeman, each of whom checked part of the text and offered invaluable comments.

From the first meeting through to subsequent correspondence, Richard Browne gave me excellent cooperation from his crossword editor's desk at *The Times* (though this book is not an official *Times* publication).

Last but not least, my thanks to Isabel Read at HarperCollins whose help to me as a novice author at all stages was invaluable.

I have not mentioned the support of my wife of over 40 years, Pamela, because, in keeping with her usual style, she asked me not to.

Index